Parenting for Character

For Sara, Therese
and Mayumi

Parenting for Character

Equipping your child for life

Andrew Mullins

Scepter

Published by Scepter Publishers, Inc.
info@scepterpublishers.org
www.scepterpublishers.org
800-322-8773
New York

Parenting for Character
This edition first published in Australia and New Zealand by Finch Publishing

Edited by Kathryn Lamberton
Editorial assistance from Rosemary Peers
Text designed and typeset in 10.5/14pt Esprit by Anna Warren, Warren Ventures
Cartoons by Cathy Wilcox
Cover design by Steve Miller – 154 design
Cover photograph courtesy of alamy.com

ISBN: Paperback 9781594173783
ISBN: eBook 9781594173776

Notes The 'Author's notes' section at the back of this book contains useful additional information and references to quoted material in the text. Each reference is linked to the text by its relevant page number and an identifying line entry.

Disclaimers While every care has been taken in researching and compiling the information in this book, it is in no way intended to replace professional medical advice and counselling. Readers are encouraged to seek such help as they deem necessary. The author and publisher specifically disclaim any liability arising from the application of information in this book.

Contents

Introduction

'Good character consists of knowing the good, desiring the good, and doing the good … habits of mind, habits of heart, and habits of action.'

DR THOMAS LICKONA, STATE UNIVERSITY OF NEW YORK, CORTLAND

Build good habits if you want your child to be happy

Character equals good habits. If you are systematic and persevering in sculpting good habits of thinking and acting in your child, you will have a happy child and a happy adult. You must carve these habits from the living rock of a deep and loving respect for others. With such habits your child will thrive in adult life. Parenting is less about looking after the now, and more about preparing children to take control of their *own* future lives and to connect with others in lifelong relationships.

Never forget that you are sculpting for life. This is the essence of parenting for character.

Provided food, shelter and family love are not lacking, happiness in adult life is largely determined by the good habits we have in our character – habits of optimism, generosity, honesty, loyalty, self-control and clear-headed problem-solving. It is upon our own habitual behaviours and attitudes that the relationships we form will flourish or flounder.

Happiness does not depend on feelings, or on what others do or don't do, so do your best to raise your children so that they are not tossed around by impulsive reactions – outbursts, overeating, putting things off, dominating fears, grudges that destroy – based on passions and emotions working to their detriment. Raise them so that their good intentions are not thwarted by ingrained habits of laziness. Raise them from their youngest, most formative years with a sure sense of what will enrich them as human beings, and with the courage to walk away from anything that will diminish them or lead them to use others for their own gain.

My experience is that parents who keep their focus on these priorities, patiently and lovingly, give their children something of incalculable worth. *The Talmud*, a type of ancient Jewish guidebook for life, sums it all up: 'The one great requisite is character'. Plutarch, the famous Greek historian writing in Roman times, knew how to cut to essentials: 'Character', he wrote, 'is simply strongly established habit'.

The Don on character

'When considering the stature of an athlete, or for that matter any person, I set great store on certain qualities which I believe are essential in addition to skill. They are that that person conducts his or her life with integrity, courage, and perhaps most of all with modesty. These virtues are totally compatible with pride, ambition and competitiveness.'

Sir Donald Bradman, 1908–2001

Habits for happiness

A child needs:

- *habits of sound judgement* guided by an accurate understanding of what is right and wrong, and of what enriches and degrades a human being
- *a deep sense of responsibility to others and well-tried habits of generosity* if he or she is to be capable of forming and maintaining permanent relationships
- *self-possession and habitual self-control*, conferring a relative freedom from internal weaknesses and bad habits
- *resilience and habitual toughness* in the face of difficulties or difficult people
- *common sense and courage* to resist external pressures from the media or peer group
- *to develop the wherewithal to be an effective parent when his or her own time comes.*

Get the behaviours *and* the underlying motivations right

It's not difficult to make children happy – just take them to McDonalds, or put them on a PlayStation. That will make them happy – *now*. But that is not the end point of parenting.

It is much more important to equip the young people in our care to find happiness *as adults*.

There are *two* simple ingredients in this process of equipping children for adult life. They are universal principles. The great writings of the East, classical literature, the great books of the religions, all emphasise these perennial co-constituents of good parenting:

- Children need a clear understanding of what is right, founded on clear reasoning and deep respect for others – *values*, or *conscience*, if you prefer that word.
- These values, in turn, are the foundation for well-grooved *habits* of responsible behaviour.

On these co-principles parents have successfully raised children since Adam and Eve got it right with Abel. The happiness of children and – let's not forget it – of parents themselves has hinged through every culture and age on having strong habits driven by loving motivation.

Habits need good values. Habits alone are insufficient. Stalin and Genghis Khan had well-developed habits of *action*, but little conscience ... the results were horrific.

Nor are good intentions enough. Think of the times you have hit the snooze button, fibbed to get out of a fix, left the sink untidy, eaten too much. Our values gnawingly remind us what was best for us; when we fail in behaviour, we lose our peace of soul, and our happiness. Don't confuse values with good habits. They are not the same.

Character education will not be achieved through sugary bedtime stories or by videos of rainforests. In your own family, a parental focus on building good habits will equip your son or daughter not only with wisdom and peace in their hearts but the capacity to act as they really wish to. Your aim as a parent is to consolidate in your child these life-skills – *virtues*, to use a word that now labours under excess baggage – in the deepest sense.

In this book we will focus on building up these *good* habits, habitual behaviours motivated by a loving and responsible attitude towards others.

Testimonies to the importance of developing good habits

Found throughout this book are insights into other cultures, times and places that serve to demonstrate the *universal* wisdom of various principles in raising children, most particularly the importance of cultivating the full range of strengths of character, good habits and virtues.

'Behold I give you these useful counsels
For you to ponder in your heart;
Carry out these things and you will be happy.'

ENY, AN EGYPTIAN SCRIBE, ADVISING HIS SON TO FOSTER VERY SPECIFIC BEHAVIOURS, SUCH AS HONESTY, KEEPING GOOD COMPANY, BEING INDUSTRIOUS, REMAINING ACTIVE, PRAYING, AVOIDING FORWARD WOMEN AND CARING FOR HIS FAMILY

'A youth, when at home, should behave well toward his parents, and when abroad, respectfully to his elders. He should be earnest and truthful. He should overflow in love to all, and cultivate the friendship of the good. When he has time and opportunity, after doing those things, he should study the polite arts.'

CONFUCIUS, 551–479 BC

'Life is short so keep thyself a simple and good man, uncorrupt, dignified, unaffected, a friend of justice, god-fearing, gracious, affectionate, and manful in doing thy duty.'

EMPEROR MARCUS AURELIUS, 121–180

'There is no truth more thoroughly established than that there exists in the course of Nature, an indissoluble union between virtue and happiness.'

GEORGE WASHINGTON, 1732–1799

'All sober inquirers after truth, ancient and modern, pagan, and Christian, have declared that the happiness of man, as well as his dignity, consists in virtue.'

JOHN ADAMS, 1735–1826

'The true Christian, product of Christian education, is the supernatural man who thinks, judges and acts constantly and consistently in accordance with right reason illumined by the supernatural light of the example and teaching of Christ; in other words, to use the current term, the true and finished man of character.'

POPE PIUS XI, 1857–1939

Assess your child's character

There is no definitive number of qualities of character. Thomas Aquinas listed over 200 but the consensus is that these distil to four key habits (in bold type on pages xiv–xv), followed by the main associated habits. This list reflects the work of David Isaacs, an English Professor of Education.

Use the table to reflect on the range of positive qualities of character that your son or daughter possesses and those in need of further development. You may wish to photocopy the pages and tick the boxes. The differing perspectives of both parents are important, so ideally sit together and discuss each quality in turn. Work as a team.

Remember, habits need good motivations. How easy it can be for all of us to fall into the trap of working hard, but for selfish materialistic reasons. For behaviour to be good, it must be motivated by a loving intention. The columns under A and B correspond to these co-principles of a happy life.

Under 'Current level of development', consider how frequently your child manifests a specific behaviour. Under 'Motivation', look for objective indicators that reveal the motivation for the behaviour. Consider, for example, if your child's words show that the behaviour is *other centred* or whether it is evidently *self-seeking*. Consider also if motivation is *intrinsic* or *extrinsic*: is it being driven more by internal convictions or by external rewards and praise?

After you finish working through columns A and B, discuss the priority areas for attention in your son's or daughter's character. If you see that, too often, your son's or daughter's motivation is self-centred, you may decide that the development of loving motivation is itself a priority area.

You will find these qualities discussed in more detail in the pages that follow, and you may well refine many of your initial observations. That's perfectly okay. Your parenting really should be dynamic and responsive to new observations and new insights. Fear only complacency and loss of focus. You have been given no more important task than to raise your child to the very best of your ability. Whatever you do, keep your eyes on the ball. Too often parenting comes unstuck because parents, just like kids on a Friday afternoon in the classroom, get distracted.

The purpose of this book

Parenting for Character is a manual for building good habits in children. It is not an arbitrary list of tips but a practical framework for sound parenting. In the process of parenting for character, we adults also need to look at our own habits, so be ready to assess your own character and your own parenting, and remake those habits that need to change. We would be hypocrites to expect children to improve themselves if we saw no need to lift our own game.

To change any behaviour requires clear goal-setting and dedicated effort. And the older we get, the more humility we need if we are to change the way we do things. Too often our impatience with our children, or our own lack of engagement with them, says much more about our own lack of character than about the child's. Rather sobering, I know.

Using *Parenting for Character*

- Asterisk the best advice you come across in this book.
- Bounce ideas off your better half, if you have one.
- Work through the assessment pages.
- Discuss and decide upon very specific parenting resolutions. *Fix on three or four family resolutions*, goals that, if they are achieved, will make your parenting more effective.
- *Write them down.*
- ***Review them together each month. This is the most important step.***
- Be committed to make any changes necessary in yourselves, individually, and as a team, to make your parenting more effective.

	A. Current level of development		
QUALITY OF CHARACTER OR GOOD HABIT	***Shows this quality readily***	***Sometimes apparent***	***Rarely demonstrated***
Sound judgement			
flexibility			
understanding			
loyalty			
audacity			
humility			
optimism			
Responsibility			
obedience			
sincerity			
orderliness			
Self-control			
modesty			
moderation			
sociability			
friendship			
respect for others			
simplicity			
patriotism			
Fortitude			
perseverance			
industriousness			
patience			
responsibility			
justice			
generosity			

B. Motivation			C. Priorities for the year
Carries out these actions habitually out of love for others	***Occasionally can act in this way out of love for others***	***Often carries out these actions for self-interested motives***	***Tick the boxes beside priority points of focus for individual child***

We try to teach our kids values
Of course! How else will they know when's the right time to buy?
Wilcox

PART 1
Parenting foundations

Principles of raising children with character

'Aim to raise young men and women who can solve their own problems in life.'

Rafael Pich, father of sixteen, founder of OIDEL, a Geneva-based non-government organisation serving family rights in education

It is hard to escape the conclusion that parenting has lost much of its effectiveness. The sad reality is that the Big Day Out generation often finds it hard to cope with commitment, responsibility for others, the lure of wealth, stable relationships, and channelling its own lifestyles into paths to benefit others, and yet a failure to do so leads to serious unhappiness. There is no shortage of classrooms of happy primary school kids, but something comes unstuck too often at adolescence, just when the challenges of life should be confronted with the most idealism. We are finding it harder and harder to raise happy, fulfilled adults, equipped for the challenges that life will throw at them.

It is as if we don't know *how* to teach children to be happy as adults. We attend to their current needs but we don't look ahead. We are very good at providing an affectionate and safe environment, here and now, for a child, but *too often we don't manage to foster the strengths of character children will need in adult life*. We are not teaching that happiness depends on good habits … and this is tragic.

The dedication of parents is not in question. But we focus on *micro-parenting* at the expense of raising children with the full array of character qualities. *Much of the popular know-how in raising children has become focused on the short term* – how to deal with pressing issues, how to avoid tantrums, how to talk to an adolescent, how to change a nappy. A look at the parenting shelf in any bookshop verifies this. This micro focus *must* be matched by a commitment to build up the child's habits of behaviour. On a child without good habits 'a hard rain's gonna fall'.

No amount of time on PlayStation will make your child more ready for life. Too often we allow ourselves to be diverted into over-providing children with the non-essentials of life and under-providing on character coaching. At best our efforts are reactive rather than proactive.

We get mixed up. How is it that we can spend ourselves and our money unstintingly on children but fail to pass on the key lessons about happiness? The first law of perennial parenting has always been and always will be: *the more you love your children, the less you 'do' for them and the fewer material trappings you give them.* Surely a parent's aims are to raise children to think for themselves, to understand that happiness is in people not in things, to be fully capable of independent responsible action, and to be ready to give and receive love. If these qualities are to be in place at eighteen years of age, even the youngest child needs to be laying the foundations now. Yet something as simple as a television in the bedroom of a twelve-year-old can so easily build bad habits, not good habits.

The following pages focus on eleven core principles for raising children with character. I have observed time and again their importance, and some of the finest writing on character education returns time and again to these themes. A self-assessment checklist will follow at the conclusion of this section.

Successful parents

'Successful parents realise that children grow up not when they can take care of themselves but when they can take care of others and want to.'

JAMES STENSON, SCHOOL PRINCIPAL AND AUTHOR

1 Create unity in the home

'May heaven grant you in all things your heart's desire – husband, house and a happy peaceful home. There is nothing better in this world than that man and wife should be of one mind.'

HOMER, *THE ODYSSEY*, C. 700 BC

United parents are more likely to raise their children effectively. Studies demonstrate that the 30 percent of Australian children not raised in a home with both natural parents are more likely to suffer disadvantage on every indicator: psychological, academic and socioeconomic. The same is true for children exposed to chronic discord. Of course, a single parent or a step-parent can do a terrific job … but it is much harder.

James Stenson in *Upbringing* insists that unity is the first characteristic of successful parents. Ray Guarendi echoes this principle. He writes in his classic study, *Back to the Family*, 'the best thing a husband can do for his children is to love their mother'.

It's not rocket science. When parents are unhappy, children are unhappy. Children mirror their parents' moods. And it is a sad law of human behaviour that we are more likely to find fault in others when we are unhappy with our own situation. While pre-teen children blame themselves when mum or dad is shouting, teenagers lose respect for their parents. In either case, parenting is compromised. Beyond all this, unhappy children are more at risk of anxiety and depression, and the experience of domestic aggression all too easily resurfaces in the child's own adult behaviour. And there is a further problem. Even the sweetest children will divide and conquer to get what they want when parents cannot agree on expectations. I have seen one parent whose permissive expectations seemed calculated to bribe the children for their loyalty and to undercut the estranged partner's standards.

Two homes are never better than one. Mum and dad may form their own new homes, but the children remain itinerants. And the alternative, to ask children which parent they wish to live with, is invidious. Every child has a *right* to a settled upbringing in his or her own loving family but how often things don't seem to turn out that way.

The effects of disunity

On my first day of teaching in 1979 in a new suburb in the west of Sydney, the new recruits were told: 'One thing you must realise about this school is that 80 percent of our families are in crisis. This colours everything we do here.' It did. I spent only nine months at that school, but in the 25 years since I have never encountered children so hungry for attention, so grateful for affection and so difficult to guide.

***

Barbara Holborow, the former Children's Court magistrate, says that about 85 percent of children entering the juvenile justice system come from broken homes.

Conflict is sapping by its very nature; parents in conflict lose focus on proactive child-rearing. Teenagers are changing so quickly that parents must not take their eye off the ball. Worst of all, when parents divorce, the message to children is that love runs out, that unconditional acceptance doesn't happen in reality. In a world where their parents have rejected each other, children sense that they too can be rejected.

How to apologise – an indispensable life skill

- *Always be the first to apologise after an argument.* Certainly, never go to bed without patching up. Apologise for the things you said that hurt, and for not listening to the other person's point of view. We all need to lose the paranoia about being taken advantage of if we apologise.
- *By your own example, teach your child how to apologise.* It is better for parents not to argue in front of children, but in any case let them see you apologise. And learn to apologise to your child as well when it is warranted … for your impatience, for hasty punishments, etc. A child who knows how to apologise has acquired the life skill to restore relationships. We all need this skill in abundance.

2 Build up habits of affection with each child

'Interpersonal rewards (time and affection) are more important than material rewards.'

DR PAULA BARRETT, DIRECTOR OF THE FRIENDS PROGRAM FOR YOUTH AT FLINDERS UNIVERSITY

One father was telling of a conversation with his seven-year-old boy who had a new baby brother.

'Dad, who do you love most?'

[Pause]'… Mum.'

'No, I mean which of the kids? Who do you love the most?'

'Chris, I love you the same as your brothers and sisters.'

'Who do you *really* love the most?'

'I love each of you *exactly* the same.'

It needed to be said.

'Do you love me?' is a key question on every teenager's mind also. Each child has different needs, but *all* children do better when mum and dad are very affectionate with them.

Parents themselves can be carrying bruises. They themselves may have had a cold father, or enjoyed minimal home life, or be saddled with a matter-of-fact temperament that does not easily show feelings. But each parent has a duty to change him or herself to provide the unconditional love and encouragement children need. If not, the consequences can be far reaching. Barbara Holborow observed that the great majority of children who came into her courtroom lacked affection in their homes. And someone once wrote, 'What we do to children, they will do to society in their turn.' The stakes are high.

> *Be high on affection and on direct and clear expectations. It's as simple as that. 'Every piece of research on effective childhood socialisation identifies two broad parameters, emotional support (affection) and limit setting …'*
>
> PROFESSOR DON EDGAR, RMIT CENTRE FOR WORKPLACE CULTURE CHANGE, FORMER DIRECTOR, INSTITUTE OF FAMILY STUDIES

Build *habitual* ways of showing affection

- Ensure there is good *one-to-one time* with each child, each day – as simple as sitting on the bed to chat at bedtime.
- One parent says, 'Find something that your child and you both like, and do it together.'
- Author Dr Ross Campbell says parents need to learn to give each child *focused attention*, with *eye and physical contact*.
- Paula Barrett advises of *the importance of being positive and encouraging*, and avoiding negative refrains. She warns against an over-reliance on negative consequences and on cold-shouldering as a means of discipline.

Affection always wins

Jimmy, four years old, came down almost formally to see his mother one afternoon to announce, 'I don't want to be in this family anymore.'

Juliette could sense that something was coming as this child did tend to think outside the box: 'Oh, really Jimmy. That's a shame. Why?'

*'Well, I can't say f*** when I want to.' Jimmy's breadth of vocabulary had earned too many time-outs for his liking.*

'But what are you going to do? Where are you going to live?' Juliette asked.

'Oh, I'll live here, but you guys will have to go.'

'What are you going to eat?' responded the voice of common sense.

'I'll just get a banana from the bowl, you know,' Jimmy reassured her.

'But who is going to give you cuddles?'

This one brought on a big pause before he could respond. 'Hmmm, I think I've made a mistake.'

Jimmy didn't much use the offending word after this exchange … at least not as much.

DILLON AND JULIETTE, PARENTS OF JIMMY, THEIR SEVENTH CHILD

Emotionally nourish your teenager

In *How to Really Love Your Teenager*, Dr Ross Campbell reminds parents that it is their responsibility to 'emotionally nourish' their children. It is wrong, he says, for parents to look to children for their own emotional support.

3 Have high but reasonable expectations

'Have the courage to demand greatness from the children in your care.'

Fr Chris Riley, Youth off the Streets

'She always seemed to me like a child who had had little asked of her.' This teacher was describing a child with woeful work habits. It is a parent's duty to present challenges to a child systematically, incrementally, kindly, firmly, and with real accountability.

Children who have little asked of them and a lot given to them will be totally under-prepared in life, yet too often today we are seeing children bereft of the character development they need to cope with the pressures that society, the media and the peer group are constantly exerting.

Challenge children in all the core life-skills – in attitudes of humility, kindness and respect, and in habitual behaviours of sincerity and generosity, self-control, courage, industriousness and responsibility to others. Tailor your demands to each child's capacity, and don't compare one child's performances with those of a sister or brother. Every child has unique qualities and unique limitations.

Try not to confuse a protective environment with one that is indulgent. There is only a limited time to prepare children to face very real challenges. Try to balance the duty of not exposing children to dangerous influences with the need for a less and less sheltering environment as teenagers grow. Even younger children must learn to face problems with fortitude and inner conviction. Time is short.

Apply the African proverb, 'Don't carry a child after it can walk.' Mum and dad shouldn't be doing what children are capable of doing for themselves. Set the bottom line at a very healthy height where membership in the family implies that all members put others before themselves, work hard at responsibilities, learn to control their own temperament, contribute to family life and are generous with their things. In all these areas the best parents lead by example. One parent says, 'Start young in teaching a child that the family home is everyone's home so it is everyone's responsibility.'

Ask of each child at his or her level

- As parents, agree to ask a great deal of your children in every area – socially (building up confidence, communication skills and leadership skills), artistically, physically, ethically and spiritually.
- Ensure that your children have afternoon and evening timetables which are followed.
- Insist on their full effort in their studies; application is the focus, and the marks will look after themselves.
- Ensure that their holidays and weekends are constructive and active.
- Do projects with them so they learn to put initiative into recreation, rather than fall into habits of wasting time.

At some point your child must become a self-starter. The goal of good parenting is not to harass children to do the right thing, but to equip them to run their own lives. We all must learn to push ourselves. Example is again crucial. John Paul II spoke of his own father's example: 'My father never had to be tough on me because he was so tough on himself.'

The top 1 percent

Today in the West we are at the most affluent pinnacle of existence. Without doubt we are among the most comfortable 1 percent of the 85 billion persons estimated to have lived on this planet, so it is little wonder we must take extra precautions to ensure that we do not raise committed little materialists.

Be prepared for curly questions

Answer this question, posed by one shrewd fourteen-year-old:

'Mum, if practice makes perfect, and no-one is perfect, why practise?'

4 Lead by example

'Example is more efficacious than precept.'

SAMUEL JOHNSON, 1709–1784

It is an axiom of human existence that we imitate those we admire. Thomas Jefferson put it simply, 'Man is an imitative animal.' With young people in our care we must strive to be the very best example we can be in every facet of our lives.

From their fathers, boys learn how to live as a man, not ancient macho nonsense, but life-skills: fidelity to one's family, resilience before difficulties, respect for all women, work as service, etc. In the same way, what girl will succeed if her mother is unable to teach her the beauty of womanhood? From whom will a girl learn of the feminine co-contribution to culture? Who else can model for her the unique centring role a woman plays in the family?

Yet in teenage years, in many homes, mother and daughter clash constantly, and dad and his fifteen-year-old son are not particularly close mates. Sometimes both have even stopped trying.

On parental example

'It's amazing how high some parents put the crossbar for their kids and how low they put it for themselves.'

JACK GIBSON, A FOUNDER OF MODERN RUGBY LEAGUE

A parent's core responsibility is to give children the best head start – most of all through strength of character. The best fathers and mothers in history have not just had good communication skills, they have also had something to say; they have not just been present, their presence was a striking influence on their children. These times are no different. Parenting is not about breadwinning and cooking. It is about staying connected with children in order to teach wisdom and foster the highest habitual behaviours.

Can you tick these boxes?

Do you model these qualities for your child?

- ☐ a loving attitude towards all, present or absent
- ☐ readiness to serve
- ☐ sincerity and uncompromising commitment to the truth
- ☐ spiritual depth
- ☐ a sense of fun
- ☐ uncompromising courtesy
- ☐ self-control
- ☐ the habit of thinking before acting
- ☐ sense of responsibility
- ☐ personal toughness and resilience before adversity
- ☐ a facility for loyal friendship
- ☐ a spirit of industriousness
- ☐ a professionalism that sees work as service
- ☐ a positive and optimistic view of the world.

'All parents damage their children. It cannot be helped. Youth, like pristine glass, absorbs the prints of its handlers. Some parents smudge, others crack, a few shatter childhoods completely into little jagged pieces, beyond repair.'

MITCH ALBOM, *THE FIVE PEOPLE YOU MEET IN HEAVEN*

Example out of all proportion

Dad, you like to put your feet up as you read the paper, but soon you find yourself chipping your son because he puts muddy shoes on the leather lounge. Your occasional liking for a television program in the evening becomes an uncontrollable obsession for the seven-year-old. Batten down for the withdrawal wails! Your habit of not putting things away when you arrive home is adopted by your teenage son. In desperation, all you can do is insist his bedroom door remains shut.

And Mum, you might loathe the regimentation of having dinner ready at a particular time, but soon you realise that punctuality is definitely not your son's strong suit and your daughter keeps everyone waiting when the family is driving somewhere.

Where did these behaviours come from? A harmless well-controlled behaviour in the parent seems to have been adopted by the son or daughter without any sense of proportion or moderation.

5 Create customs of close parent–child communication

'When one of my sons comes home and I realise something is on his mind, I put on the kettle and I tell him a good story.'

MRS COSGROVE, OBERON, 1985

Your aim is to be a major player in the world of your child or teenager. You must not become marginalised by your other activities, by lack of exposure, or by a failure to connect. Strong habits of communication are essential parental habits:

- **Affection** Look at your customary ways of interacting with your child or children. Do you take a lively interest in the interests of each child? Do you share in the things that make them happy and the things that make them sad? Do you show affection by respecting your child's autonomy and privacy? Do your children share in the joy you feel in being with your family and your husband or wife? Do you easily make and accept physical contact as a sign of affection?
- **Relaxed, one-to-one listening and talking** Do you listen with your eyes as well as your ears? Do you go down to your son's or daughter's level? Do you take the time to speak deeply? Do you try to have a good chat with each child at least weekly? Count up your one-to-one conversations over the past month. You might be in for a shock. And don't count monosyllabic replies to the standard 'How was school today?' as points on your scorecard. There has always been only one answer to that question!
- **Doing things together** Try not to do a job alone. Get out of the habit of doing things *for* your son or daughter; only do things *with* them. Try not to go on car trips alone – not even to the shops. Use regular trips to Saturday sport to have a chat. Find ways to stretch out the moment – buy an ice cream and sit in the park. Above all, learn to use common activities to *listen*. Dads, particularly, have to

work hard at this. Build a bridge to your son. Read up on your child's hobbies and sports. Plan combined projects – making billy carts, fishing rods, robots, dolls' houses, you name it. How else will you ever know what your child is thinking?

'There is frequently more to be learnt from the unexpected questions of a child than the discourses of men, who talk in a road, according to the notions they have borrowed and the prejudices of their education.'

JOHN LOCKE, 1632–1704

Indelible communication

'Daddy, did you know my teacher is actually 114 years old?' my six-year-old Annie announced.

Now Mrs Bristow-Smith could not be that age – close perhaps – but not THAT old, I thought.

*'Really?' I responded with astonishment. Annie's teacher can do **no wrong** in the eyes of this extremely loyal charge. 'That must make her the oldest teacher on earth. She must be older than Santa Claus himself.'*

*'You don't believe me, she **is** 114 years old. Mrs Bristow-Smith said so!' And with that Annie stormed off in a huff crying as she ran upstairs.*

Some many months later, I thought I'd test the water. Over Saturday lunch I read aloud from a newspaper that Australia's oldest woman had died at the age of 111.

*'Well, **she is not as old as Mrs Bristow-Smith,**' Annie restated with even stronger conviction, accompanied by a look in her eye that made me wince.*

'Daddy, my teacher knows everything. Did you know animals are kind to each other, cats to cats, dogs to dogs?' Annie announced, no doubt to once again enlighten me from the wisdom of that *114-year-old teacher. 'Did you know that Mrs Bristow-Smith once saw a green frog pick up its dead baby frog and bury it under some stones?'*

'Yes, that's right, animals are very kind and caring to each other.' How could I not concur?

And the next time I want Annie to go to sleep or do as she is told, it won't be, 'Wait till I tell Santa', it will be 'Do you want me to write a note in your diary for Mrs Bristow-Smith to read?' She obviously has far more influence on this six-year-old than anyone else.

ABRAHAM AND CORINNA

Communicate more

- *'What absurdity to think of an infant bonding with a daycare worker instead of its mother. Be at home when children arrive after school.'*
- *'Don't just talk to your child, don't just listen; you must hear what your child is saying.'*
- *'Every family watches too much TV.'*
- *'Don't make the mistake of only finding moments of quality time for your child ... give your child lots of time. There is no substitute for the attention of Mum and Dad.'*

QUOTES FROM BARBARA HOLBOROW

Sticks and stones will break my bones,
But words will break my heart.

Tender age is no guarantee that charity does not give way to creatively stinging insults: an eight-year-old girl announces to her classmate, 'Even our dog doesn't like you'.

Do your level best to teach universal respect.

The price of poor communication

Our then-eight-year-old son had been nagging us for a pet mouse. We had consistently told him NO, but one afternoon he came home with one, purchased from the pet shop with money he had saved. As the only parent home, I decided to let him keep it on the basis that he cared for it completely himself. If there were any problems, it would go to a friend of his who was breeding mice. However, I failed to communicate this to my husband, who on coming home and being presented with the mouse, immediately insisted it be returned to the pet shop. Of course my son insisted: 'Mum said I could keep it.' A certain degree of friction ensued!

My son did keep the mouse. It lived for three weeks before succumbing to a foot disease (as mice do), which required a visit to the vet (costly, as vets are)! And guess who paid for that?!

JEANETTE, MOTHER OF FIVE AND VARIOUS PETS

6 Manage the inputs

'We always like best whatever we first experience … and therefore youth should be kept strangers to all that is bad.'

ARISTOTLE, 384–322 BC

The younger the child, the more impressionable. We are all drawn back to our first experiences – we look back with affection on the sports we played, the places we holidayed, the older people who took an interest in us. What a pity when those early experiences have been less than positive, or have produced in a child a liking for the mediocre, the ugly, the cynical or the selfish.

Billion dollar industries are built on turning our children into efficient little consumers. Parents and teachers do well to exercise careful management of the inputs touching the lives and minds of the impressionable young people in their care … peer group, television, the Internet, teen magazines, even the refrigerator, all leave their imprint. Children will be manipulated by anything and anybody to whom they are exposed, sometimes to their tragic detriment.

Monitor electronic recreations carefully. Computer games, unrestricted TV viewing, curiosity on the Internet, mind-numbing loud music, are all the more habit forming because of their appeal and their repetitive nature. And be warned, the smutty banter on some radio stations is definitely not fit for impressionable ears … God knows whose ears it could be good for!

More importantly, be a high impact player in the life of your child. If you know how to chat with your son or daughter in these years, you will effectively pass on attitudes and values which will stick for life. Lay strong foundations for adulthood. Everything you say is going in! Don't underestimate how much even tiny infants absorb from what they hear and see.

When all else fails, open up *Lord of the Rings* and read to your kids. Teach the fun of a good book, remembering Mark Twain's warning, 'Those who don't read good books have no advantage over those who can't read them.' That goes for parents too.

The Classical approach

'Shall we just carelessly allow children to hear casual tales which may be devised by casual persons? We cannot … therefore it is most important that the tales which the young hear first should be models of virtuous thought.'

PLATO, 428–348 BC

'Remove indecent pictures and speech from the stage and from the sight and hearing of the young.'

ARISTOTLE, 384–322 BC

The Marxist approach

'I find TV to be very educational. Every time someone turns on the TV, I go into the next room and read a book.'

GROUCHO MARX

Think about the inputs

- Do you get used to *arbitrary* influences in your homes and haphazard values, e.g. unchecked television?
- Do older siblings give a good example?
- What example is coming from print and electronic media in the home? At school? At friends' homes?
- Do you have effective management of the peer group influences on your children? Do you give effective leadership and guidance in these matters? Have you found a school where the input from staff is always positive, and from peer group predominantly so?
- Do you create an atmosphere where quiet reading and study are valued at times in the home? Or is your child over-stimulated by noise and disconnected images?
- Do you always talk to your children about any negative inputs to which they are exposed, for example, some news reports? Do you see your role as that of giving clear criteria about what is good and bad in those inputs?

The power of electronic media

- *Andrea (Year 3): 'I saw the video, I know how the world will end.'*
- *Dylan's parents did not know he had watched* Armageddon *21 times.*
- *Will (Year 6) has 185 computer games on his bedroom shelf.*
- *At Monday morning news, a Year 3 primary school girl says earnestly, 'I saw four videos on the weekend. Videos are my life.'*
- *'Why don't you give up TV for Lent?'*
  'I'd rather die!' says eight-year-old Stephanie.
- *Teacher: 'What's your favourite video game?'*
  *Year 3 boy: '*Mortal Kombat III*'.*
  Teacher: 'Killing people!'
  Year 3 boy (smiling): 'Kids like that sort of thing.'
  (Two months later) Teacher: 'Which game are you playing now?'
  *Year 3 boy: '*Twisted Metal.*'*
  Teacher: 'Sounds violent.'
  Year 3 boy: 'No, it's not violent ... people get run over and blood comes out.'
  Teacher: 'It's not violent?'
  Year 3 boy: 'No, it's not violent ... you get to use lots of weapons. Remotes are my favourite. They have dynamite. The people scream when you kill them.'
  Teacher: 'It's not violent?'
  Year 3 boy: 'No, it's not violent.'

Never underestimate the power of a story

*Pre-teen children are like sponges. One morning a seventeen-year-old repeated to me **word for word** a moral story about a certain Rufus and his nemesis Brutus that I had made up as his class teacher when he was seven. Then he asked me what happened next!*

Promote quality reading and screen out trash

'It was wrong of me as a child to prefer empty romances to more valuable studies.'

AUGUSTINE OF HIPPO, 354–430

7 Let your child wear his or her mistakes

'Children need to fail. When we impulsively protect our children from failure, we deprive them of learning.'

MARTIN SELIGMAN, *THE OPTIMISTIC CHILD*

Society is full of kind-hearted parents who cannot do enough for their children. What could possibly be wrong with this? Surely this teaches children to be kind to others.

It can be a serious misjudgement for parents to do things for their children which the children are able to do themselves. Don't shield kids from the small difficulties that they experience. Do intervene in situations of moral or physical danger, but don't fight their battles for them, if they can safely fight them themselves. Don't run to their protection if they are oversensitive. Don't write 'Please excuse John from his homework because he left his book at school'. Children must learn to solve these small problems so that they have the capacity to solve their own problems in adult life.

Robert Louis Stevenson wrote, 'Sooner or later we all sit down to a diet of consequences'. If we don't hold children to the natural consequences of their actions, they may well be in much more trouble later. It is vital that young people are required to lie in beds they have made. A child who forgets his lunch comes home a little hungrier. He won't forget it tomorrow. It is better for children to be penalised for a late assignment in primary school than to be awarded zero for a Year 12 assessment task.

Nor must we over-manage senior students, who in the eyes of the law may already be adults. We must not defend them from consequences of their actions, particularly if the situation can provide a lesson for the future. This is essentially why schools must not go soft on drugs. Actions have inevitable consequences. All young people must learn this rule of life; the earlier they do, the less pain there will be.

Kindheartedness out of control

A lady is carrying her son's schoolbag and several large bags of shopping. Beside her is her seven-year-old son trotting along with nothing in his hands. A few moments later, her son halts at an ice-cream counter. Mum walks on, and then gestures urgently, 'Come here!' Son gestures back just as urgently, 'Come here!' Mum retraces her steps and buys an ice cream for the boy to carry. This is real life.

***

One father objects, 'My son is a fussy eater, but he is not spoiled.' Perhaps he is right, but only a little time later the same parent looks fondly on at cricket training while the ten-year-old shows a remarkable working knowledge of crude vocabulary. Dad does nothing to correct the budding linguist.

A night to remember

A local shop owner rang to tell us he had caught one of our ten-year-old students stealing lollies. The teacher who knew the boy best spoke to him about stealing, organised for him to face the shopkeeper to apologise, and encouraged the boy to speak to his father about something as important as this. The boy went pale.

The next day the boy's father, absolutely grateful and ecstatic, rang the school. He said, 'Alex grew 6 foot last night.' He and his son had never had such a good talk.

What that young man didn't know was that the teacher had rung his father to say, 'Don't get angry. Your son has something important to tell you tonight. Give him the opportunity, try to listen first and only then talk. Don't overreact.'

Eight years later in his last months at school, the boy wrote about that talk with his father as one of the greatest moments of his childhood.

We teach our children *not* to say 'Sorry'.

*Instead, we teach them to say, '**I** am sorry'. There is a big difference. There is personal responsibility involved. And we try to model that way of talking ourselves.*

Trev and Jodie, parents of three.

8 Place a high priority on honesty

'Honesty and transparency make you vulnerable. Be honest and transparent anyway.'

MOTHER TERESA, 1910–1997, NOBEL PEACE PRIZE 1979

Children who do not learn to respect truth may deceive others; they may cheat and steal. More seriously, they may deceive themselves. When children get into the habit of escaping the reality of things, of not facing up, they are deprived of the machinery to identify and remedy problems in life. A child who always has excuses is taking the first step to irresponsibility in adult years. A child who learns to be honest is laying the foundations for fulfilling relationships and friendships, for professional reliability and, most importantly, for peace of heart.

In my experience, a child who is still having problems with sincerity when he or she is eight or nine years old will often have a big task ahead. Already habits of insincerity will be quite ingrained. Parents and teachers with children like this should try to pick up every little insincerity. There are far too many children who, in teenage years, have a serious problem in facing reality … and this possibly could have been avoided by the greater diligence of parents and teachers in earlier years.

Older children have a long aerial for hypocrisy. It is very obvious to a teenager when adults bend the rules for themselves, when they put on an image in front of visitors, when they talk badly behind backs, when they like to be noticed, when they expect children to work hard at school but don't mow their own lawns. Socrates proclaimed, 'People hear what we say but follow what we do.' Well, heaven help the children of hypocritical parents; their parents will be of little use to them. It has been claimed that in one Western city the average citizen tells one lie every eight minutes! Socrates would have had something to say about that.

'The only time I have ever been angry with my children is when they have not told me the truth.'

JOSEPH, FATHER OF BOYS RANGING FROM 21 TO 4 YEARS OF AGE

Be aware of the possible causes of a child's insincerity

When you find your seven-year-old has been spending ill-gotten change on bubble gum cards, or when your daughter goes to see a different movie from the one she tells you about, it is a heaven-sent opportunity to help you understand why your child has a problem with sincerity:

- First, look at yourself. Are you an example of absolute integrity?
- Look at overreactions. Does your child fear you? If you contort in apoplexy when your son dents the car, how will you react when your daughter falls pregnant? If you *readily* lose your temper, make a resolution now *never* again to lose it with your children. A one-off loss of temper is neither here nor there, but a parent who is chronically hard to please and critical creates an adolescent who can be unreachable.
- Are you overbearing? A parent who is dogmatic, who talks *at* children, who spends more time talking than listening, or who puts himself or herself up as an example, will find children frustratingly reluctant to open their hearts.
- Do you rely on punishments to teach lessons rather than on reaching the heart of your son or daughter? Do you keep things in proportion or do you exaggerate issues? Do you punish your child more when they own up, or do you have the sense to mitigate the punishment when a child is sincere? When your daughter confesses in confidence to you, do you talk about it in front of others in the family?
- Are your punishments arbitrary and irrational? Do you listen to your child's version of events before determining a punishment?
- Is your child receiving a bad example from friends who are used to hiding things from their parents?
- Be aware of a child's temperament and how it can affect sincerity. Some children have more closed personalities, or can even be agonisingly sensitive. Others have proud and perfectionist personalities. They don't like being wrong and find it hard to apologise. Either way, this child is better off learning to open his or her heart when young. In a few years a relationship may depend on it.

9 Enjoy family life

'A strong family life is the solution to all of society's problems.'

RAFAEL PICH, FATHER OF SIXTEEN

Ask yourself these questions and, if you think your family life is lacking, try to do something about it. It is crucial to your child's healthy development:

1. Is our home an enjoyable place? Are we creative in organising fun family activities each week?
2. Do we enjoy the company of our friends and do we allow our children to join in?
3. Do we realise that the mood in the home depends on our faces? Do we create a peaceful and cheerful environment by our habitual good humour?
4. Do we control our appetites and emotions? Do we strive to ensure that our own self-centred behaviours don't hijack peace in the home? Remember, when parents are stressed or cranky, younger children blame themselves.
5. Do we model deep, mutual warmth and affection between ourselves constantly? Do we each spend one-to-one time with each child each day? There is no substitute for the personal attention of a parent. Children will learn from anyone who spends time with them but lessons from a parent are indelible … that's the way nature works.
6. Is home emotionally stimulating? Do we talk affectionately and provide plenty of reassuring physical contact? Do children sense that the great priority of their parents' lives is to be with family?
7. Is the home environment rationally stimulating? Are we careful about the images, sounds and conversation we put in front of our child? Do we model wide interests and openness to new ideas? Do we model enthusiasm? Do we talk passionately about idealistic issues or do mundane and materialistic topics dominate?

8 Do mealtimes and bedtimes give a basic order to the day? Are there clear daily routines? Do we strive to create family customs of self-discipline – putting things away, not snacking between meals, sensible TV and computer game regulation, etc. Routines and reasonable expectations make it easier to teach responsibility without nagging and without depressing the atmosphere in the home.

9 Is the physical environment bright? Do we do our best to keep things habitually tidy and clean? Are things left higgledy piggledy around the house? Do the adults and older children leave things in the sink? Do we all clean up after ourselves?

10 Do we see family mealtimes as a daily set play in which we can educate our children in ways of looking at current events with idealism, compassion and respect for others? Do we model optimism?

11 Do we scrupulously avoid any negativity? Keep smiling … we are not in this for ourselves! Do we teach our children to look at issues objectively, and to make a plan to overcome every challenge?

Consensus on family life

'All the misfortunes of men derive from one single thing, which is their inability to be at ease at home.'

Blaise Pascal, 1623–1662

'There is no doubt that it is around the family and the home that all the greatest virtues, the most dominating virtues of human society, are created, strengthened and maintained.'

Winston Churchill, 1874–1965

'By far the most important channel of transmission of culture remains the family; and when family life fails to play its part, we must expect our culture to deteriorate.'

T S Eliot, 1888–1965

Family jokes smooth out anxious times

There is a blonde joke (yes, a very typical blonde joke) which tells of a blonde with a Walkman who asks the hairdresser to snip carefully to avoid dislodging her earphones. Finally, the creation is complete and the hairdresser goes to get the mirror to show her the back view, but removes the earphones to do this. Immediately the lady collapses. Oh no, what's the matter? No response! Start CPR. The ambulance arrives, and the lady is revived and taken to hospital. In the excitement, the earphones have been pushed aside and a young apprentice is sweeping the floor when she comes across them. She picks them up and listens. What do you think she heard? 'Breathe in … Breathe out … Breathe in … Breathe out …'.

This silly joke works wonders at all sorts of times:

1. *Before a party, one of my children (early twenties) is sooooooo excited that she is really not able to help with the preparations, let alone greet guests, etc. All I need to say is 'Put your earphones on!' and she laughs and calms down.*
2. *Tim came home recently and said someone at school had called him 'blond' (no, I didn't ask). The next day he was off to do a university aptitude test. He was to drive himself, didn't know the way, and was a little anxious about the test. I wanted to give him a hug before he left. That was not going to be accepted! So I said, 'Now you're a blond you can take the earphones with you!' And I got the hug!*

Cathy, mother of four

Go straight to the heart

Every word of what you say must be true, or you are using cheap emotional blackmail:

Example A: 'John, you really let mum down this afternoon when she had to ask you three times for help to bring in the groceries. You know how much she does for us both. Mate, you cannot do that again. To make up, I want you to go and apologise and ask if there is something you can do for her now.'

Example B: 'I understand that you are upset, and that you feel ripped off, that you think we no longer love you, and that the world is against you. I understand you go a little crazy every now and then … but you still have to put out the garbage.'

10 Be convinced that love and correction are not opposites

'If the people are governed by laws and punishment is used to maintain order, they will try to avoid the punishment and have no sense of shame. If they are governed by virtue and rules of courtesy are used to maintain order, they will have a sense of shame and will become good as well.'

CONFUCIUS, 551–479 BC

Do you remember Mr Wilson in *Dennis the Menace*? He wails, 'In a tragedy of such proportions, someone must be to blame.' Perhaps there is a little of Mr Wilson in all of us. Sadly, if we are prone to blaming and if we resort to angry and resentful performances, we will scar children. Do not harp on negatives. Do not cultivate guilt. Do not correct in anger.

Does this mean we should not punish children? Not at all. The word 'punish' may bring back all sorts of memories for each of us, yet without punishment, lessons sometimes do not stick. Simone Weil, the young woman mystic of occupied France, proclaimed that 'punishment is a vital need for the human soul'. The key is to punish children *without* the histrionics. Love and correction must be inseparable – the calmer, the better. Model self-control and be positive: once the punishment is applied the slate is wiped clean. The mistake is forgotten. The more punishments are the natural consequences of an action, the better. If a child racks up a large mobile bill, the child pays. Don't get angry, but do get the money.

Punish only out of love

Aquinas said, 'Punishment is a forceful discipline applied to educate a man to take his part in orderly social life.' Punishment must *always* be medicinal. The aim of sanctions is to educate, not to get someone back, or to get even, or even to make of someone an example. Your love must be obvious, so don't punish when you're angry.

Minimise the need for punishment by a home culture characterised by kindness, clear expectations and realistic, well-monitored goals. The best teachers and parents follow these principles, and address each child very personally. Indiscriminate punishments are a cop-out. A child must be helped to internalise lessons, to accept responsibility, and this must happen personally. Punish *and* explain the lesson, particularly teaching how the child's negative behaviour affected others.

There should be a clear link in a young person's mind between the punishment and the actions which attracted that punishment. Just as praise must be very specific, blame is only acceptable when it, too, is very specific. There are no bad children, only bad actions.

And who said punishments can't ever be fun? A little creativity goes a long way to helping children understand that corrections are a necessary part of life. Some children in Year 2 at my school so liked picking a job from the Box of Doom in their classroom that they talked their parents into punishing them in the same way at home. The more mistakes they made, the more lucky dips they got!

Some mantras for discipline

- The earlier, the easier.
- Supervise. Sidetrack. Stop.
- Calm, consistent, with consequences.
- Preparation (inform beforehand of the consequences); separation (loss of a privilege); reparation (the child makes right what he or she has done wrong).
- Clear, concise and change the subject.
- Only chase once!

A life principle

'Don't accept tripe!'

SARAH MAY, 95 YEARS OF AGE

The purpose of correction cannot be to make a child do the right thing ...

'This is what a father ought to be about; helping his son to form the habit of doing right on his own initiative, rather than because he's afraid of some serious consequence.'

TERENCE, 190–159 BC

'Imposing things by force is not the right way to teach. The ideal attitude of parents lies more in becoming their children's friends ... friends who will share their anxieties, listen to their problems, and help them effectively and affectionately.'

JOSEMARIA ESCRIVA, 1902–1975

When a correction is too harsh ...

Thirteen-year-old Jake was being particularly painful one day at football training, horsing around and not putting his heart into the drills. Finally the teacher exploded. Jake was sent packing in no uncertain terms. The next day, the teacher looked for him, 'Jake, I'm sorry. I should not have been so angry, but do you realise why I was upset?'

'It's okay sir, I have to be corrected.'

A win, definitely a win!

Parents have always had to hold the line

Found on an archaeological scrap heap in Egypt:

'Dear Father.

How can you think of not taking me to town?

If you won't take me to Alexandria, I won't write to you, or speak to you or greet you!

If you go I won't hold you by the hand, or ever speak to you again if you won't take me! ...

It was so nice of you to send me lovely big presents ... Do please send me a lyre. If you don't I won't eat or drink. So there!

Theon.'

11 Commit to building good habits in your son or daughter

'It makes no small difference whether we form habits of one kind or of another from our very youth; it makes a very great difference, or rather all the difference.'

ARISTOTLE, 384–322 BC

Human behaviour does not materialise from cyberspace ... our individual actions normally manifest the patterns of behaviour that are established in our personalities as second nature. So a person who has a *pattern* of honest behaviour, even when pressed, will normally tell the truth. A habit of study makes it easier to pass exams. A habit of problem solving means we do not lose our serenity when we walk into a house that has been burgled. But a person with a *pattern* of irresponsibility, in a crisis, will find it hard to hold jobs and relationships.

So much adult behaviour derives from habit: good habits of industriousness, responsibility, honesty, or debilitating habits such as eating disorders, habitual emotional outbursts, deceptions, impulsiveness, etc. Habit makes easier the good actions that make us and others happy; and bad habits cause us to fall short of our potential and frustrate our desires for happiness. Character, at its core, is a mix of good and bad habits, each with the self-centred or other-centred intention that underpins it. A good habit motivated by love for others is nothing other than a virtue.

Habits are acquired by repetition of actions, yet all too often we find ourselves entrenching poor behaviours without even realising it. Our default mode is to entrench bad habits. Have you ever noticed that cabin crews on international flights all have their own distinctive culture, varying even within the same airline – some go the extra yard and some are simply slack? How easily people can import into their own make-up the hard-nosed behaviours towards others they see around them. The way human beings work, if we do not strive for a positive habit, is to groove a negative trait.

And habits are incredibly durable. Good habits acquired by a child will travel with that child through life. Bad habits can dog them through adult life. Some say it takes 30–60 days of focused determination to change a habit. Psychologist and author Michele Borba claims that it takes a child 21 days of repeating a new behaviour before it takes. While these numbers can seem simplistic, the reality is that habits are very durable, for better or for worse. And just when we have overcome a bad habit, be it smoking, laziness or lying, we find ourselves relapsing. Tiredness too can easily bring back to the surface a negative trait we thought we had mastered.

All of this has *profound* implications for raising children. A child who is encouraged to pattern good behaviours in his or her personality will have acquired these strengths for adult life. A child who is raised to be habitually reflective, fair, industrious, positive, cheerful and self-disciplined is much more likely to make a success of professional life and future relationships. Parents who focus on developing in their child the full range of virtues put their son or daughter well on the road to self-confident, loving adult life.

Attention Deficit Disorder

There is no medical consensus on the family of behaviours grouped around the term, Attention Deficit Disorder (ADD). What can be said is that everyone needs to develop strong habits of self-control for adult life. Combined with any decision to medicate or not to medicate, and any strategies to set clear boundaries etc., must be a concerted, consistent and sustained effort to help the young person involved develop the range of behaviours they will need in adult life. Every child needs to learn to respect others; every child needs to develop self-control. ADD cannot become an excuse for a lack of respect for others, or for irresponsible behaviour. It may provide some explanation, but never an excuse. For our own peace and happiness in adult life we must have established habits of self-mastery.

Assess your own parenting

Harder than forming good habits in your son or daughter is *changing your own habits* – the concrete has been setting for a lot longer.

Are you ready to change?

- Are you ready, as parents, to be co-responsible for your child, to work as a totally unified team, or at the very least, in all matters relating to your parenting?
- Are you ready to give a first-class example in everything? Your child will mirror your actions and attitudes, and more importantly your deepest values.
- Are you ready to look constructively at your own parenting skills?

Your own happiness and the happiness of your family depend on your readiness to grow. So look at the values that motivate you most deeply in life:

- Is parenting a key task in your life mission?
- Do you believe that your fulfilment and happiness are interwoven with the success of your parenting?
- Are you determined to raise your children to have good habits of mind and action no matter what personal sacrifice is involved?

If you find this quite confronting, it might be a good idea to ask yourself why. In any case, I hope this doesn't stop you from receiving the message of this book loud and clear.

Complacency is the doormat of disaster

A former school captain of my school returned from a semester of tertiary study in another Western country. The lack of focus in parents he came across during the trip amazed him: 'They were just not giving importance to really obvious things like knowing what their children were doing when they were not at home. They were incredibly complacent.'

If you have decided to go on, sit down on your own and work through the various items in the table on pages 32–33, ranking your performance. Then pass the book to your husband, wife, partner, or even your non-cohabiting co-carer if you have one, to rank you on the same topics. When comparing notes, be prepared to take a small step towards self-knowledge. Reflect on the old adage: 'The best business in the world would be to buy someone for what he is really worth and sell him for what he thinks he is worth.'

> *'A good person demands of himself. A petty person demands of others.'*
>
> CONFUCIUS, 551–479 BC

> *'To change one's life: Start immediately. Do it flamboyantly. No exceptions.'*
>
> WILLIAM JAMES, 1842–1910

Parenting foundations

POINTS FOR REFLECTION

- Parenting *starts with* and is *sustained* by the love of mum and dad.
- The loving relationship of parents creates a culture of loving relationships in the home.
- Affection between adults and between adults and children may be natural but it also requires ongoing effort to show habitual signs of affection.
- Expectations determine performance. Let us not stunt the development of children.
- Example always works.
- Family relationships thrive on frequent, honest communication.
- Damaging influences in the life of a young person can drown out family ties.
- Don't fight children's battles if you can coach them to fight their own.
- The dedication of parents makes family life really enjoyable for each family member.
- Character will grow through example, advice and timely, affectionate correction, provided parents have a clear vision of the habitual strengths that they are seeking to foster in their son or daughter.

ASSESS YOUR PARENTING QUALITIES

Unity between parents ... in expectations, and in cooperation, and in frequent communication
Affection for each child ... independently of the child's good or bad behaviour
High but reasonable expectations
Readiness to give a good example in everything, at all times
Customs of close communication with each child
Effective management of the influences coming into the lives of the children
Readiness to ensure that children accept the consequences of their mistakes and faults, provided they will not be harmed by these consequences
A high priority on honesty in your home, in your own behaviour and in your children's behaviour
Creativity in family life – a readiness to ensure that each weekend, from the time your children are young, you plan enjoyable family times together
Habitual cheerfulness – cheerfulness that does not depend on external events, but rather on the peace of soul within you
A will to correct, with affection, but clearly and urgently
A determination to build good habits systematically in your children, presupposing a deep awareness of the needs of each child

Level of development					Priority areas
Well-developed	***Fair to middling***	***Fair***	***Much work needed***	***Non-existent***	

Fine. So tell me exactly what it is you want me to think for myself.
Sigh...
Wilcox

PART 2
Good habits – the building blocks of character

Not one *more* theory of how children should be educated

Benefits of habits of good behaviour

Repeated behaviours become second nature

We are the sum of our established habits

Good habits and parenting

The four powers – foundation habits for happiness

1. Sound judgement
2. Responsibility
3. Self-control
4. Fortitude

Importance of a spiritual dimension

Review your child's good habits

'Silver and gold are not the only coin; virtue too passes current all over the world.'

EURIPIDES, C. 480–406 BC

In this section we look in more detail at the link between good habits and character. This comprehensive and systematic way of looking at parenting has been largely lost to our generation, but such a focus will give your child a head start of inestimable value.

Not one *more* theory of how children should be educated

World literature for at least the past 2400 years has been permeated by a vision that the worth of a person's character may be gauged by the established qualities in his or her personality – cheerfulness, responsibility, trustworthiness, and so on. Such good habits, or virtues, have always been seen as the traits of character that enable a person to act effectively in and on the world around them, and they have been seen as essential for the self-determination on which peace of soul and happiness hinge. And parenting has been seen as the process for developing good habits, or virtues, and in turn character, in young people.

Origins of the word

Virtue derives from the Latin *virtus* (strength) which is based on the word *vir* (man).

Almost every major classical writer subscribed to this. One can hardly turn a page of Homer, Plato, Cicero or Virgil without finding references to good habits as key constituents of character. Aeschylus, Sophocles, Euripides, Thucydides, Aristotle, Horace, Tacitus, Plutarch, Seneca and so many others shared the same vision.

This world view was picked up throughout the entire canon of pre-twentieth-century Western literature: from Old English *Beowulf*, pre-Renaissance Dante, Elizabethan Shakespeare, to Jane Austen, Manzoni and Tolstoy. All assess personality and character in terms of virtue.

Joseph Pieper, a prominent twentieth-century philosopher, described this vision of character as '... one of the great discoveries in the history of man's self-understanding, and has continued to be part and parcel of the European mind ... the result of centuries of persistent intellectual endeavour by all the creative elements of the emerging West, both the Greeks (Plato, Aristotle) and the Romans (Cicero, Seneca), both Judaism (Philo) and Christianity (Clement of Alexandria, Augustine).' No small praise.

Furthermore, this vision of human flourishing is found not only in the West. Practically every other culture has made the link between happiness and good habitual behaviours, although without Aristotle's clarity of argument. Consider the traditions of the Jewish people in the *Book of Wisdom*. And from Ancient Egypt there are beautiful documents preserved linking consistent virtuous behaviour with happiness. It is true also in the great writings of the East: contemporaneously with Socrates, Confucius was teaching of three universal virtues: wisdom, love and courage.

This two and a half thousand year understanding of the link between good habits, character and happiness has been discarded in the past 50 years, but at what cost? Is this one reason for the relatively high failure rates of parenting today? In fact, in any age, has this failure to inculcate habituated strengths of character been the mark of ineffective parenting? Certainly my experience of twenty years close work with hundreds and hundreds of parents and their children convinces me of the incredible benefits that flow from systematic and persistent attention to the development of good habits.

Benefits of habits of good behaviour

'Virtues … a kind of health of the soul.'

CICERO, 106–43 BC

The benefits of establishing habits of good behaviour in your children include:

1 **Freedom** Do you notice that from time to time some rogue behaviour, such as laziness, pessimism or vanity in talking about yourself, jumps on board and hijacks your good intentions? Or do you find yourself manipulated by external pressures – the company you are keeping or the opinions you hear on talkback. The antidote is to establish *counter* habits of thinking, choosing and acting the way you wish to, so that you are truly self-directing and free to choose what you know to be best for yourself. Good habits confer freedom.

2 **Abiding love for others** The *habit* of commitment underpins loving relationships – generous, loyal, clear-headed, selfless, sincere ways of interacting with others in our lives. Mutual commitments are uniquely human. Pet cats are not up to commitments that will provide their kittens with a stable family upbringing. But even human beings' *promises* of commitment are not enough if they lack the necessary *habit* of commitment; *intentions* can unravel when life picks away at them. Habits and intentions are not the same thing.

So much of our happiness depends on knowing ourselves to be loved wholeheartedly, uniquely and *permanently* by another. Yet, to qualify for the commitment of another, we must be capable of giving ourselves utterly. Teach your children to honour commitments, to keep their word, to face up to consequences of the simplest actions, otherwise when commitments become adult sized their good intentions may not last the distance.

3 **Moral maturity** Kids grow up, but some fail to *mature*. Maturity is not about age. Think of maturity as the integrated and harmonious development of the spectrum of good habits enabling us to act freely and to love others. When we read comments on school reports like 'Siegfried lacks maturity', does it surprise us that there is work to be done to even out his character? Schools should not see themselves as galleries of completed masterpieces. Yet the same lack of maturity in an adult is a worry: a 25-year-old careless of others, habitually dishonest and not able to be told is dangerous for everyone. One Roman schoolteacher drew the line between moral behaviour and habit 2000 years ago. He wrote, 'Moral virtue comes about as a result of habit'. Take your child out of the showcase, and work hard at polishing his or her character now.

The discovery of happiness

Aristotle was the first person to explain happiness. He said that happiness hinges on the good habits, which he called virtues, which we have incorporated in our character.

Lasting happiness is founded, he said, not on power, pleasure or even, in a direct way, on relationships. Aristotle proclaimed, 'Happiness is the reward of virtue.'

He explained this idea in the *Nicomachean Ethics*, a book many think he wrote for his son, Nicomachus.

It would be unwise to suggest that this vision of character development is just one more opinion about the way a human being ought to mature. Aristotle's *Nicomachean Ethics*, as it is known to us, is not just another book on the parenting shelf; it is without doubt one of the great texts of civilisation.

We disregard such a patrimony of civilisation at our own peril because an understanding of virtue, good habits motivated by love, has always brought with it a certainty about where happiness is to be found. To discard this heritage is somewhat akin to torching the library of Alexandria, an act of chaos and ultimately of self-harm.

Repeated behaviours become second nature

'Habit, my friend, is a practice long pursued,
That at the last becomes the man himself.'

EVANUS, A GREEK POET

Repeated actions create habits, which are *short cuts* to action. These manifest either in a physical sense (a tennis forehand, or even a skill in dicing carrots), or in a moral sense (habits of keeping calm in a crisis, controlling one's eating habits, being orderly). This simple insight has had profound consequences for parenting.

While these short cuts are not sufficient in themselves to bring happiness, they are, you could say, the building blocks, the DNA, of happiness. Add an underlying love for others motivating these actions and the cocktail is complete.

All our habitual actions should be guided by reason. It is too easy to take on habits that are not good for us. Aristotle explained the link between habit and virtue. He wrote, 'There are three things which make a person good and virtuous: one's natural endowments, one's habits, and one's determination to act in accord with what is reasonable and good for a human being.' In other words, our efforts to develop good habits should be guided by what our reason tells us is good for us. So it would be silly to pursue order in the garden shed at the cost of constant arguments.

Compare Aristotle's three principles with our simplistic vision of personality derived from 'nature and nurture', or nature and habit. Aristotle is so far ahead of us. We have left out *reason*. Aristotle reminds us that our habitual actions must be guided by *our own* true reasoning, as well as reflective convictions, if they are to make us happy. We need to base our decisions on objective principles such as 'Do good and avoid evil', 'Do unto others as they would do unto oneself', 'Life is always a great good', and so on. A person who lacks moral convictions is a ship without a rudder; there is no moral compass. There is no *conscience*. As a civilisation we have only a blurry understanding of the critical role that a person's own reason must play in educational maturing. This is a serious defect in our present assumptions about parenting and education which, I believe, is making it harder for us to educate children in critical thinking and self-control.

For this reason, sound judgement, the habit proper to our intelligence, was described in ancient times as the 'chariot driver of the virtues' – holding the reins for all our other actions. This will be discussed in more detail on pages 49–50.

Our habitual actions sum up the sort of person we are

The worth of our lives comes down in many ways to the quality of our habitual actions. Compare a person who is habitually self-centred with one who is habitually thoughtful.

All our actions impact inexorably on our personalities. By our habitual actions we really decide the sort of person we want to be. Aristotle understood them as those features of character that make us good people, in the broadest sense. He said, 'Virtue in man is a state of character which makes a man good, and which makes him do his own work well.' Habit, for better or for worse, is the dominant ingredient in our personalities.

Bullying

Attempts to deal effectively with individuals who bully others should focus on remaking habituated bad behaviours, not just through one-off corrections, but by insistence on sustained repetition of sound behaviours and on encouraging the need for loving motivation for all actions – two key principles in ensuring good habits. Counselling for individuals suffering from bullying requires an insistent focus on the need to forgive, and on strategies for building up habits of resilience by assertively directing the person to stop annoying actions, focusing on external behaviours and not judging the other person's intentions, solving recurrences by going to the right person for help and showing self-restraint to respond to words only with words.

We are the sum of our established habits

'We become just by performing just actions, temperate by performing temperate actions, brave by performing brave actions.'

Aristotle, 384–322 BC

Pam Stenzel, in delivering her 'Sex has a price tag' workshop to half a million teenagers each year, proclaims 'Past behaviour is the best predictor of future behaviour'. Isn't it so true that we all find it hard to break away from entrenched behaviours? Our characters are the sum of our good and bad habits with their underlying motivations. Character equals habitual behaviours.

Remember Thomas Lickona's quotation on our very first page: 'Good character consists of knowing the good, desiring the good, and doing the good ... habits of mind, habits of heart, and habits of action.' Human maturity implies that we have developed comprehensive and integrated character strengths in the three fields of action for a human being: thinking, choosing and doing. Nurture your child's character to this end.

Dale Carnegie spoke of '... four ways, and only four ways, in which we have contact with the world. We are evaluated and classified by these four contacts; what we do, how we look, what we say and how we say it.'

While it is true that he focuses specifically on habits of action, externally manifested behaviour, the ultimate message is the same. We either develop good *habitual* behaviours in these areas, or we will be deficient as human beings.

Isn't it all too much for a parent to keep focused on the ongoing development of these various spheres of activity for each child in his or her care – to be regularly monitoring how effectively the child thinks, judges and acts? Lighten up! Surely it is a lot easier just to let a child's character *unfold*.

The problem is that *character* does not unfold. Only our *personalities* unfold, with their unique blend of genetic qualities, interests and mannerisms. The development of character requires, and always has required, conscious focus. Parents who do not actively engage in helping a child make the consistent *efforts* needed to develop their full range of qualities will let that child down. What sad and avoidable mistakes children fall into in adult years because their parents did not help them to think calmly or to make decisions unskewed by emotion. What mistakes because parents did not teach habits of self-control and of humbling themselves to apologise, or accept an apology, when a relationship is in the balance.

The state of the world is the sum of the behaviours of all of us who are in it

Ultimately, Aquinas explained, peace and order in society will be a reflection of the peace and order in our hearts. So much negative behaviour in the world around us derives from personal failures of character:

- Lack of solidarity with developing countries and exploitation of their workers.
- Selective respect for others leading to ineffective correctional systems, cultures of disregard and torture, lack of regard for the aged and the vulnerable, lack of will to find alternatives to abortion that scars women and deprives children of life, etc.
- The inability of leaders themselves to forgive and bring their peoples to understanding, cooperation between nations, and world peace.
- The widespread breakdown of permanent relationships and the subsequent effects of this on children and on all concerned.

Top 10 qualities for strong character

These qualities are recognised and taught by nearly all philosophical, religious and cultural traditions:

1 wisdom
2 justice
3 fortitude
4 self-control
5 love
6 positive attitude
7 hard work
8 integrity
9 gratitude
10 humility.

The first four are none other than the cardinal virtues that we shall be looking at in the pages that follow.

Dr Thomas Lickona,
Character Matters (2004)

Good habits and parenting

'... habits – established patterns of thinking and doing things – that all successful families have in common.'

STEPHEN COVEY, *THE 7 HABITS OF HIGHLY SUCCESSFUL FAMILIES*

Clear-headed and effective character education does not happen by chance. It implies:

- a clear vision of the type of young man or woman you are raising
- a systematic effort to engage in the development of the full range of qualities your young person will need
- a commitment to self-improvement in each parent
- a desire to model a loving intention with utter constancy.

We either aim for the complete package, or we settle for something vastly inferior. Unless we teach children that happiness is in effective habits of thinking, choosing and acting, they will not discover this by chance. No number of monkeys on typewriters will ever come up with *War and Peace*. Unless we teach children that happiness and permanent relationships derive very much from building up a loving intention in all they do, they are unlikely to discover this. And we know what proportion of relationships fall apart in our society.

Parents are facing a great deal of competition in raising their children, competition from the peer group, from the media, from the bad example of role models in society. If in the face of that pressure, parents abrogate their responsibility to raise their children well, children will suffer. A good parent, an effective parent, does not throw in the towel.

There has been much written in the past fifteen years about virtue education. Many prominent overseas writers have now published on this theme. Former US Secretary of Education, William Bennett, published the bestselling *Book of Virtue*, and followed it up with *The Moral Compass*. Professor Thomas Lickona's *Raising Good Children* and *Character*

Matters are impressive arguments for the happiness that strengths of character bring. Canadian Dr Donald DeMarco's *The Heart of Virtue* is a delightful collection of stories illustrating the love that must underpin good habits. And William Kilpatrick's chilling analysis, *Why Johnny Can't Tell Right from Wrong*, should be required reading for all parents.

But Australia is lagging in this important field of virtues education. Only Melbourne couple Gerard and Margaret O'Donnell's practical guide to the work of Professor David Isaacs, *Family Values*, is a standout.

Are you raising your child to be good?

Fewer people now overtly aim to raise *good* children, as if *good* were not in the best interests of the child, or because *good* can seem such a relative term, or perhaps because as a goal goodness can seem to have a high disappointment rate. Based on the mistaken impression that *good* is first of all a religious evaluation, many parents and educators avoid using it, or aiming for it.

But of course *good* is a moral term, and morals are defensible on *rational* grounds, a crucial clarification.

Consequently, as our society has become increasingly secularised, we have disregarded the rationally defensible and ultimate goal of parenting, to teach children to live a moral life. Cicero described it as the way of living *most suited* to our nature, most able to bring us happiness: 'the habit of living in the way most suitable to our human nature, guided by what is reasonable'.

Parenting has lost its universal standard, and in the process, it has lost the capacity to raise children to be happy adults.

Serving others brings out the best in us

'Looking after these handicapped kids for three days does more good for a young person than weekly counselling for five years.'

Fr Chris Riley, Youth Off The Streets, talks of his programs that have street kids caring for handicapped children

The four powers – foundation habits for happiness

'Why are these old philosophers so up-to-date? Because they took their bearings not from the date – nothing is so quickly dated as the up-to-date – but from the unchanging essence of man, the inherent structure of the soul. Plato was the first to discover and map this … The four cardinal virtues … are relevant to man in every age because they are relevant to man himself, not to the age. They fit our nature and nature's needs.'

PETER KREEFT, PHILOSPHER

As we saw in the Introduction, all qualities of character fall under four broad headings:

- sound judgement
- responsibility
- self-control
- fortitude.

These foundation habits for happiness have been known for two and a half millennia as the four *cardinal virtues*. The breakdown almost certainly goes back to Socrates, and is found unanimously in Plato, Aristotle, Cicero, Augustine and Aquinas.

This division is not arbitrary. The four span the major spheres of action and interaction with others. Virtues are all about self-management. By these four foundational strengths

Perennial bullet points

In an ancient history essay, my niece wrote: 'Aristotle taught the boy Alexander two major lessons: the importance of observation, and the doctrine that the mind must control the body if one is to be capable of effective action.' Quite a challenge to summarise the contribution of the greatest philosopher in two bullet points!

The wisdom is perennial. If we are to set our own course, and not be buffeted by wayward emotions, mischievous media and problematic peer groups, we will need to anchor our world view on objective facts and use our head, not our feelings alone, to direct our actions.

of character we gain the facility to effectively use our intellect (the great power of reaching the truth of things) and our will (the principle of choice and action, empowering us ultimately to love). For more on the psychology, see the boxes on pages 47 and 48.

Sound judgement and self-control are internally directed and give us the necessary strengths to manage our mind and our passions.

Responsibility and fortitude are externally directed, empowering us to live up to our duties towards others and to overcome external difficulties.

It is important to cover all four bases. A child who is courageous but who has little self-control will put himself and others at risk. A child who is prudent but who lacks justice

Rational Psychology 1A

Aristotle was the first to propose an understanding of how human beings are put together. He taught that within us all there are various integrated features:

- our intellect (our power to understand)
- our will (the power to choose and to love)
- emotions and passions (feelings and driving forces in our lives)
- our senses
- habits of behaviour which we have developed for better (virtues) and for worse (vices).

The consensus since Aristotle has been that, in a well-balanced personality, intellect should govern will. *Head should guide heart.* Choices should be based on a good understanding of the situation.

Normally our intellect, helped by accurate information from our senses and sound convictions and reasoning processes, should guide the judgements and choices of our will.

Emotions and passions are closely linked to our senses, but also need the guidance of reason. We are a package deal: our happiness is linked to using our reason to manage our choices, our passions and our emotions. Ultimately, all our actions may be traced back to considered or impulsive choices, to well or poorly managed passions and emotions.

will end up looking after number one very effectively. We cannot overestimate the importance of these four habits: they are the four powers by which the greatest men and women of all times have been able to manage themselves effectively and serve those they love.

Rational Psychology 1B

Aristotle and Aquinas taught that human nature experiences seven passions: love and hatred, desire and fear, joy and sadness, and anger. A major challenge for us all is to manage these often wayward passions and feelings so that we can think clearly, and then direct them for our good. The four cardinal virtues are the key habits that give us effective management of our thinking, and of our passions and feelings.

Passions and emotions are good in themselves but in need of guidance if we are to draw strength and benefit from them; otherwise they act independently on the will and can short-cut our intellect. When passions and emotions pre-empt decisions, we can end up doing things that we don't want to do, or that are not good for us – we love the wrong things, we eat too much food, we fear things irrationally, we allow sadness to dominate our moods, we give into bursts of impulsive anger, etc.

Of the four cardinal virtues, *sound judgement* refers to effective management of our thinking. But the other three help us manage our passions and feelings so that our passions and feelings do not manage us.

For example, without *self-control*, our passions of desire or anger could dominate our decision-making. Without *fortitude*, our fears could stop us thinking clearly, and without *responsibility* to keep our self-love in check, our decisions could neglect our duties to others.

In a well-rounded personality, through these four habits we maintain a dominion over our passions, using them for good, but not surrendering to them.

1 Sound judgement

'There is clearly nothing we should be more concerned to cultivate than the power of forming right judgements.'

ARISTOTLE, 384–322 BC

This habit gives us effective management of what is happening in our minds. 'Happiness depends more on the inward disposition of mind than on the outward circumstances', said Benjamin Franklin. We cannot necessarily control external events but we can control our response to them … or we ought to.

Pattern effective ways of thinking for your own peace of mind, literally, and so you can teach these habits to children:

- Strive to discipline your imagination and memory.
- Tap into feelings and emotions. Learn to draw strength from passion, but avoid impulsive decision-making based on unreasonable reactions.
- Nurture a healthy capacity for reflection and consideration of all the factors in any issue.
- Commit to what is truly important in life, and set priorities on the macro scale (attention to my family is more important than to my work) and on the micro scale (organising myself to be home in time for dinner tonight).

'It is not enough to have a good mind; the main thing is to use it well', the great philosopher, Descartes, said. If we don't think clearly, we cannot run our own lives. Ignore the Victorian overtones of the older name of this virtue, *prudence*; by whatever name, this habit is a perennial necessity. David Isaacs says that sound judgement is the most important quality for a teenager to acquire, and for parents of teenagers to focus on. In a nutshell this is the task of parenting older children.

Teach critical thinking

The Master said, 'Anyone learning without thought is lost; anyone thinking but not learning is in peril.'

CONFUCIUS, 551–479 BC

The development of *critical thinking* is one of the most important processes for young people to learn during adolescence. It is an extension of the habit of sound judgement, *the ability to make correct decisions based on the right values*. People who think critically are able to judge and act from inner principles and conviction. They are less susceptible to peer pressure, and less prone to rash judgements and emotional reactions.

Critical thinking always starts with a solid grasp of *reality*. Teach children to look for the facts in a situation. This helps them to avoid decisions based on incomplete information, emotion or personal prejudice.

Irrationality – when the will follows emotions

We need well-developed habits in the exercise of our intellect and our will. If not, our intellect can fail to give effective guidance to our will, and we can easily be tossed around by our passionate and emotional reactions. Our decisions are then driven more by feelings than by deliberate decision-making. We act irrationally.

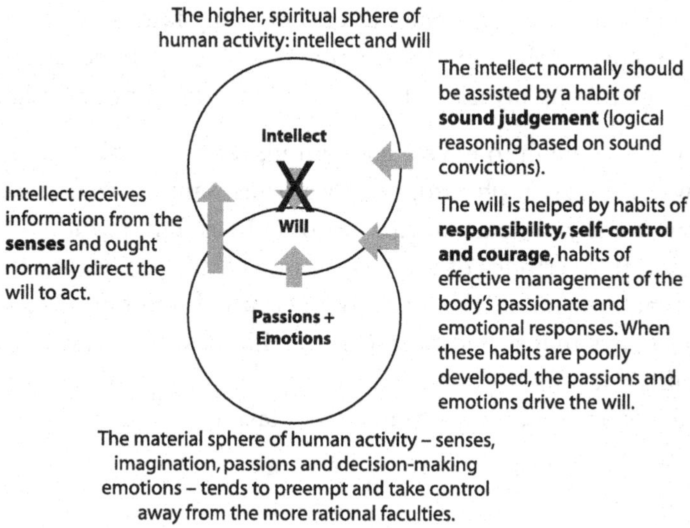

2 Responsibility

'Maturity involves being honest and true to oneself, making decisions based on a conscious internal process, assuming responsibility for one's decisions.'

MARY PIPHER, CLINICAL PSYCHOLOGIST

In my first year as principal, a parent taught me a big lesson. At least I hope I have learnt it. His child's knee had been injured, potentially quite seriously, in another boy's prank that misfired. The parent pursued me relentlessly, 'Who is responsible for the behaviour of boys in the schoolgrounds after school?' My first reaction was to duck, saying to myself: but in this case nobody is responsible because it happened in an unsupervised area, because there was no malice involved, because it was after school, etc. But that reaction is not good enough. Ultimately, whether I liked it or not, as the headmaster of the school, I was responsible. Particularly where children are involved, there needs always to be an adult who accepts ultimate responsibility. When a child lacks the age, the experience or the good judgement to look after himself or herself, parents have the duty to ensure that at all times there is some person who accepts responsibility for the care of their child. This was a very good lesson for me.

To learn responsibility we need to work up effective habits of being other-centred. Young persons today have a great many privileges: full room and board, loving parents – usually, access to education, a great variety of entertainment, relative freedom of movement, ease of communication, etc. With these privileges must come the serious responsibility of using them well. This means doing jobs for the welfare of the family, studying very hard, using entertainment in moderation and not as an end in itself, using cars responsibly, using telephones sensibly (by limiting themselves to short calls, and making sure to ask permission before using the phone), and so on.

Over two thousand years ago, Seneca wrote about teaching

children responsible use of time: 'Children should be left some free time but that should not be allowed to turn to idleness; a child must not be allowed to get used to living an inactive and idle life.' Children will only see time as a gift, and develop strong habits of service, if these qualities are modelled by the adults they admire.

These are serious issues. For example, a sixteen-year-old student who is not studying a solid two and a half hours each night is not showing responsibility in keeping with the privilege of attending school full time and thereby being exempted from other full-time work. In many other cultures and other times, fifteen-year-olds work or worked as adults. Teenage freeloading is a twentieth-century invention, unless it was your misfortune to be Louis XIV's nephew!

One word of warning. Responsibilities have to be appropriate! In the first year of my school, having only a part-time secretary, we rostered young students to answer the school phone to give them real responsibilities. One day a student picked up the phone and in his best voice said, 'Redfield College. Can you help me?' From that moment we looked for more realistic jobs to give our students!

Responsibility delivers justice

'Justice means respecting the rights of all persons. The Golden Rule, which directs us to treat other persons as we wish to be treated, is a principle of justice that can be found in cultures and religions around the world. Character education efforts often centre on justice because it includes so many of the interpersonal virtues – civility, honesty, respect, responsibility, and tolerance (correctly understood not as approval of other people's beliefs or behaviours but as respect for their freedom of conscience as long as they do not violate the rights of others). A concern for justice – and the capacity for moral indignation in the face of injustice – inspires us to work as citizens to build a more just society and world.'

DR THOMAS LICKONA, STATE UNIVERSITY OF NEW YORK, CORTLAND

Dimensions of responsibility

- honouring one's parents
- doing one's duties
- working diligently and seeing that work as service
- honouring one's commitments
- use of time
- civic responsibility
- accepting responsibility for one's actions, including mistakes and their consequences
- accepting new responsibilities as we grow
- always putting the welfare of those close to us above our own interests
- solidarity with the vulnerable and the underprivileged
- respect for others whether or not they respect us, whether or not we agree with their actions – by the very fact they are human beings accepting that they have rights and dignity.

Lost opportunities

'Monopolistic mums', to use a term of Rafael Pich, deny their children the opportunity of growing in responsibility. *'Debilitating dads'* are no better. Nor is it a good idea for parents to justify silly or superficial behaviour with a shrug and 'Kids will be kids'. This child will soon be capable of making choices that will change his or her life irrevocably. If children of ten or twelve years old are not expected to behave sensibly, they might not be able to find the common sense button when the stakes are much higher two or three years later. Then, a life might depend on it.

Prompt justice

Our eight-year-old was dawdling over his dinner as usual, after the rest of the family had finished. Our fifteen-year-old son decided to hurry him on. 'If you don't finish in five minutes, you're going straight to bed with no dessert,' he reprimanded.

When I suggested that allocating punishment was actually my responsibility as a parent, he looked at me and said, 'Well, SOMEBODY has to keep them under control!'

Jeanette, mother of five

3 Self-control

'Do not allow a child to throw tantrums. Freedom that is unrestrained, results in a character that is unbearable. Yet realise that total restriction leads to a servile character.'

SENECA, 4 BC – 65 AD

Feelings and emotions are good, but we should manage them; our feelings should not manage us. Two thousand years ago, Cicero wrote, 'Lack of self-control betrays a fundamental defect in one's mind and reason.' Human beings are still the same – either our head guides our emotional life and our passions, or we end up like Aphrodite, in Homer's description, 'the slave of her passions'. For all of his shortcomings, Nietzsche understood the debilitating effects of our passions, 'The abdomen is the reason why man does not easily take himself for a god.'

Self-control is the foundation habit giving us self-management. When we have incorporated it in our character, we more easily control our temper, we are able to delay gratification by a conscious decision, and we can say *no* to ourselves so as to check our sensual appetites and passions when they are not good for us or when they harm others. We learn to be content with pleasures in moderation. We grow in patience and exercise habits of courtesy and good manners, and generous habits of service. By growing in the ability to make apologies when they are called for, we acquire the essential life-skill of being able to restore relationships.

I once asked a mother at a parent teacher night why her son was having problems getting his essays in on time. She told me, 'I can't do anything with him, he just lies on his bed smoking marijuana!' Only years later did his younger brother tell me, 'Mum … she was the worst! She was always smoking pot!' Children with impulse control problems are, mostly, the children of parents with self-management challenges of temper, impatience, curiosity, quickness to sit in judgement of others, laziness, wasting time, disorder, even of infidelity and substance abuse. A different weakness may manifest in a child, but at the core it is self-control that has not been modelled.

So there!

'The young people of today think of nothing but themselves. They have no reverence for parents or old age; they are impatient of all restraint; they talk as if they alone know everything and what passes for wisdom in us is foolishness in them. As for the girls, they are foolish and immodest and unwomanly in speech, behaviour and dress.'

PETER THE HERMIT, 11TH CENTURY

Parents must be awake to pitfalls for a teenager: TV addiction, pornography, snacking at will, continued failure to stick to responsible study routines, sloppy habits of getting up, and of going to bed at any hour, etc. Once those habits of poor self-control become ingrained, they will work so much mischief.

It was written of Socrates that 'He very easily resisted the temptation to drink more than he needed.' There is something in all of us that admires that degree of self-possession. We recognise that such self-mastery is the mark of someone who is exceptional. And deep in our hearts we realise, too, that it probably made him happier than others around him. He was even able to make his disciples laugh on the morning of his execution. They don't come much better than this man.

A lack of self-control degrades us

'The impulses of an incontinent man carry him in the opposite direction from that towards which he was aiming.'

ARISTOTLE, 384–322 BC

'Passions and emotions must stay under the sway of reason. Rule your passion. It will command if it does not obey; restrain it with a bridle and with fetters!'

HORACE, 65–8 BC

4 Fortitude

'Men are not meant for safe havens.'

ROBERT KENNEDY, 1925–1968

Fortitude empowers us to make hard decisions and to stick to what is right in the face of difficulties. It is an inner toughness. We stay focused on a worthwhile goal rather than succumbing to setbacks, inconvenience, pain, and even our own earlier failures. *Courage, resilience, determination, endurance* and a *healthy self-confidence* are all aspects of fortitude. Setbacks, sufferings, and a refusal to feel sorry for oneself can build character.

To teach fortitude, be a source of encouragement for others, model calmness in the face of difficulties, teach your children to break problems down. Lean towards physically demanding experiences – walk to the shop with your children, take them on camping holidays, work together in the garden each weekend, create a family culture of leaving the armchair or the largest slice of the cake for the last person. And possibly the best way to teach fortitude is by passing on positive attitudes towards work.

> *'Work at home for children promotes the early maturity of children.'*
>
> RAPHAEL PICH, FATHER OF SIXTEEN

Perhaps we give lip service to hard work, but we don't believe glowingly in its importance. Does work have prestige in the family? How do you talk about work? What is your body language? Do you get far more enthusiastic about weekends or sport than work?

If mum complains about all the work she has to do, or if dad delays replacing the washer in the tap that is leaking, these messages show a distaste for work. Jimmy's homework and his report grades will suffer, sooner or later. If our aim in life is to minimise work so as to maximise fun we will never teach children that work is something good. Aristotle said that love is the inclination towards something we see is good – we will never teach a love of work unless we are convinced of its value.

We may know the theory: work enables us to do great good for others, starting with support for our loved ones; it is the instrument by which we make the world a better place and attend to the needs of those less fortunate than ourselves; it is the means whereby we develop our abilities and interests; we may even see it as a privileged sharing in the creative activity of God. But like any lesson in the home it is taught by example and directed practice.

How do we know when we over-shelter children?

Every home is a sheltered environment for impressionable children. A sheltered home or school environment buys time to inculcate good habits and convictions. That means clear guidance in what is right and wrong, managed exposure to challenges to their values, close training in responsibilities, etc.

'My Dad says you don't achieve anything unless you work hard'

The following question was asked of a number of children: 'If Dad came to you and said the family was going away for a year and you could only take one thing with you that you really wanted, what would you bring?' All but one child nominated PSII, XBox, Nintendo or a DVD! One boy said he would bring some schoolwork with him, because, he explained, 'My Dad says you don't achieve anything unless you work hard.'

What made this boy different? This boy's father *often* tells him terrific little moral stories. The boy is able to recount them word for word with great enthusiasm … and his immigrant parents both push themselves.

How are you teaching your son or daughter to work hard?

Try to see that jobs around the house are habitually done well – vacuuming the car regularly, leaving the kitchen tidy after each meal, doing repairs promptly, and so on. When parents readily step in to do jobs with their children, when they 'coach' them to finish the details, they are passing on a positive message about priorities in life.

Importance of a spiritual dimension

'Talk less to your son about God and more to God about your son.'

AN OLDER DAUGHTER'S ADVICE TO HER FATHER

Gandhi said, 'There is more to life than increasing its speed.' There *is* more than flesh and blood to a human being. The immaterial powers of knowing and of loving set us apart from all other animals.

Matter has such severe limitations! Simple observation shows us that material realities decrease as they are given away or shared, and that material things tend to break up into their constituent parts. Death is precisely this decomposition. And although material things are inherently flawed, this intuition does not defuse our shopping gene: we never have enough of material goods or pleasures, unsatisfying as they may be.

Spiritual realities follow different rules. The great intangibles of love, goodness, unity, beauty and truth manifest a world beyond the material. Love is *not used up* the more it is shared around. It is possible to deeply love all mankind, each and every last person. Unlike computers processing information, humans do not run out of disk space the more they know. Aristotle insisted on the immortality of the human soul by arguing that the soul being spiritual (not spiritual in a religious sense, but as the principle of our loving and knowing), would not decay into constituent parts. Our knowing and loving would continue. This was an awesome enlightenment for the pagan world.

'Man cannot live without love. He remains a being that is incomprehensible for himself, his life is senseless, if love is not revealed to him, if he does not encounter love, if he does not experience it and make it his own, if he does not participate intimately in it.'

JOHN PAUL II, 1920–2005

The power of prayer

'Grannie, pray for me. I have an exam tomorrow!'

'I have prayed for you every day of your life . . . of course I will.'

The boy went back to his books humbled and feeling incredibly loved.

Surely the prayer of parents, and grandparents, must be infallible. When, in professional life, an employer gives a responsibility, if he is a good employer he gives all the support needed to carry out that charge successfully. Why should our God be any different when he gives the responsibility of parenting?

'I have a very special guardian angel.'

BEN (94 YEARS OLD) SPEAKS OF HIS ESCAPES FROM DEATH ON THE BURMA RAILWAY IN WORLD WAR II

Idealism is another spiritual quality of the human personality, though, heaven knows, we seem to exercise it so little. In our hearts we must admit that mere matter, or material gain, cannot fulfil us. Ideals are the antidote to materialism. Ideals empower us to go out of ourselves, to dethrone the lounge room idol of self-interest.

Once we are attuned to the spiritual, we are awake to community and family. We cannot fulfil ourselves in isolation, no matter how hard we try. Those who do not experience the self-gift and affection of others remain tragically unfulfilled. This operates on at least three levels: the parent–child bond, the spousal bond and, for many, the creature–creator bond.

We need to build *receptors* for the vast spiritual world. We have eyes and ears for the material world, and our senses process only material information. Only dimly, now and then, we sense infinitude, *whispers of immortality*. Antoine de Saint-Exupéry once wrote, 'If you want to get a man to build a boat, do not give him wood and make him use tools, rather teach him to yearn for the immensity of the ocean.' Plato insisted that the most fulfilling action for any human being comprised contemplation of perfection and infinitude. *Silence, reverence, prayer* – these are the receptors your children will need for this other world.

What a sorry lot we are – in nature and in beauty and in truly good actions we can divine the very spirit of God, and yet we find them boring. Our hearts are restless. Nobody has taught us to yearn for immensity, nobody has taught us to contemplate. Turn on the adrenaline, turn up the volume. Pass me a DVD, plug in the iPod, check out my new phone, hurry up and sit down, *Seinfeld* is on.

Intuitions of infinity

'Our hearts are restless until they rest in thee.'

AUGUSTINE OF HIPPO, 354–430

'The Infinite Goodness has such wide arms that it takes whatever turns to it.'

DANTE ALIGHIERI, 1265–1321

'What can be seen on earth indicates neither the total absence, nor the manifest presence of divinity, but the presence of a hidden God. Everything bears this stamp.'

BLAISE PASCAL, 1623–1662

'The visible order of the universe proclaims a supreme intelligence.'

J J ROUSSEAU, 1712–1778

Faith, hope and charity ... for children

- **Faith** Show in your day-to-day priorities that you do not look to material things for lasting happiness. Teach that we are passing through this material world. Teach that God reveals himself to those who seek him. Seek him together with your children.
- **Hope** Dante said, 'Hope is certainty of things to come.' Teach that the inevitable difficulties and sufferings of life are not without meaning. God has things in hand and all will be well, if not in this life in the next. If there is such sadness in this world, how this world must be just the insignificant doormat of eternity.
- **Charity** We each have a vocation to love ... to give love and to receive love.

Good habits – the building blocks of character

POINTS FOR REFLECTION

- We do not need to reinvent the wheel. The great writers, thinkers and parents of the past have much to tell us about parenting.
- If we want our children to be *happy*, now and as adults, they need to be virtuous, equipped with good habits motivated by love.
- Be *expert* in developing the full range of good habits in children.
- Raise children to be truly free – from undue influence from those around them and from the debilitating effects of their own bad habits.
- Use routines to build good habits in children. Look critically at *routines and timetables* in your home. Repeated actions should gradually become part of our very character.
- Pass on to children an understanding of how the *spiritual and material dimensions* of our human nature interact. Teach that emotions and passions need to be guided by our convictions and decisions, otherwise they take us in directions we would prefer not to go.
- Keep focused on the *core business of parenting*: nurturing the four key habits of sound judgement, responsibility, self-control and fortitude.
- Seek *self-knowledge* – my worth as a person is measured by my habitual behaviours.
- *Respect and responsibility* are the foundation for a personality that is truly just and fair.
- *Self-control* in minor areas, such as controlling anger and getting up on time, readily transfers to greater self-management in adult life.
- *Courage* helps prevent a young person from becoming destabilised by difficulties.
- Look critically at *consistency* between parents. *Talk together often about your parenting.*
- Set *goals* for each of your children.
- Raise your children with a sensitivity for the *spiritual*. By your example teach that gratitude and humility are indispensable attributes. Rediscover the habits of prayer that you perhaps learned as a child, and pass these habits on to your own children.

REVIEW YOUR CHILD'S GOOD HABITS

Sound judgement
thinks before acting
thinks critically about television shows
thinks logically
finds out the facts before deciding
reacts rationally instead of emotionally
sets own priorities
Responsibility
accepts responsibility for own decisions
does not offer excuses
able to show hospitality
cares for own belongings
carries out allocated jobs around home
gives good example to younger siblings
Self-control
controls appetite for food and drink
controls impatience and temper
controls imagination and curiosity
manages own timetable
easily able to accept difficulties cheerfully
manages money and possessions sensibly
able to detach from entertainment easily
Courage
bounces back after setbacks
accepts correction
physically strong, tough and resilient
shows determination in the face of difficulties
shows self-confidence
speaks up against injustice

Level of development					Priority areas
Well-developed	***Fair to middling***	***Fair***	***Much work needed***	***Non-existent***	

You were right Dad – you said if we stayed at it, we'd get there in the end... Dad ?...
Pant, pant...
Wilcox

PART 3

Forging good habits

Raise children who can take control of their own lives

1 Establish routines and be consistent
2 Delegate, even if it takes more time to get the job done
3 Teach that actions should be motivated by love
4 Don't let bad habits accumulate
5 Don't do the thinking for your child
6 Model the qualities you want to pass on
7 Clearly teach what is right and wrong
8 Help your children build good habits in their younger years
9 Make character building the aim of children's sport
10 Show your children that hard lessons can be the best lessons
11 Keep focused on sincerity and generosity – habits for our heads and our hearts
12 Teach detachment from material things
13 Focus on causes and consequences

'We need to be constantly requiring children to engage in repetitive acts of generosity, industriousness or patience in order to enable them to develop these good operative habits.'

MARGARET AND GERARD O'DONNELL, *FAMILY VALUES*

In the section that follows, you will find proven approaches for building the spectrum of character qualities in children. As you read, measure your own style and home life against these benchmarks. Pick up the ideas that strike you and talk them over together. A second perspective always helps, and the efforts of both parents are crucial for success in refining home culture.

Raise children who can take control of their own lives

Keep in mind that the overall goal of parenting is to raise children to run their own lives. Children must not be made into little obedient robots – *conformity* with what you are asking is not the goal of parenting. Use every opportunity to get children to *think* for themselves, *choose* for themselves, and *act* independently by early teens. Get them ready for the autonomy that is coming. Already by their mid teens young people are making decisions that can change their lives – party drugs, sexual relationships, decisions about the priority others will have in their lives. Character needs to be in place by mid teens; challenges do not wait until you are ready.

Your son or daughter will need the full range of qualities: strengths of the head, of the heart, of readiness to overcome external and internal obstacles; in other words, the four key habits. Preferably they will require large servings of humility, optimism, industriousness and a dozen other strengths of character. Research tells us that your child will be happier and more resilient with ideals and spiritual beliefs. He or she will need dominion over feelings, but still readily draw on them for passionate dedication to important goals, and for the ability to show genuine warmth and affection to others.

Infants Give plenty of appropriate responsibilities to younger children, and follow them up calmly and with much affection. See they are fulfilled. Don't ask big things, but little duties they can handle. Remember the golden rule: what a child can do, he or she should do! Help a child always to do things out of love for others in the family. Explain the reasons even to a small child so conscience develops. Take conversation seriously. Allow consequences to take their course, and insist your son or daughter accept them. Don't fight their battles.

Primary-aged children Teach self-discipline, order and respect for others early. Take advantage of windows of opportunity for developing various virtues. You don't want to be insisting still on homework or courtesy in adolescent years; win those battles in primary school. Follow up what your child is expected to do and raise the bar each year; discuss what extra duties your child can take on. Parents should talk often about all the strengths their child will need. Be systematic. Be comprehensive in your parenting. Have strong habits of communication and of ways of showing affection.

Teenagers Require your teenagers to think critically about their own decisions but, except when it is a case of a young person walking into moral or physical danger, don't do the thinking for them. Pull back from over-managing their lives. Normally, it is counter-productive to be giving orders to a teenager. Keep the great bulk of communication light and totally positive. Correct only with affection. Know what other influences are coming into their lives and address issues as they arise. (See also Part 4.)

Now, let's look one by one at home priorities for raising children who can take control of their lives.

1 Establish routines and be consistent

'It is easy to perform a single good action but not easy to acquire a settled habit of performing such actions.'

ARISTOTLE, 384–322 BC

The building blocks of good habits in your child are the *simple timetables and routines* which you establish, and your *consistent expectations* for standards of respect towards all, and material order. The habits you encourage will be the raw material of a character with genuine depth.

Back to basics

'The older I get the more I believe in my grandmother', says Dr Paula Barrett of Flinders University.

She asks parents three questions. The first one is: 'How much sleep is the child getting?' She points out that since the invention of the electric light children are getting less sleep. The second question is: 'What are the child's eating habits?' And the third: 'What routines are in place?' 'Don't give in', she says, 'hold to the reasonable boundaries you have set'. Children need sleep, nourishing food and predictability. Get the basics right.

Parents are on the spot to see opportunities to reinforce certain behaviours, and to follow up others before they become entrenched. They are best placed to provide consistent routines, to talk between themselves to establish uniform expectations, and to agree when new responsibilities are appropriate. Their affection is crucial in helping a child work against temperamental weaknesses such as timidity and impatience.

Of course, whether you do a good job hinges on your readiness to be proactive and follow up delegated responsibilities and instructions you have given. As a builder friend insists, 'The hardest part about my job is fixing, one by one, all the small defects in the job.'

And remember, a parent's love is the key motivation for a child to do good. Not anger, not impatience, not emotional blackmail. Love.

The way we do things in our home

Establish habits founded on respect and responsibility. Just as we grew up to sayings such as 'Don't leave a job half done', establish the same explicit expectations in your family.

Recycle catch phrases for work:

- If it's worth doing, it's worth doing well.
- Work before play.
- We all chip in when there's work to be done.
- A place for everything and everything in its place.

And for interpersonal skills:

- Be the first to apologise.
- We don't shout inside the house.
- We don't talk badly of others behind their backs.
- We don't leave the table before everyone has finished.
- We give our full attention if someone talks to us.

Holiday routines

Take advantage of holidays to teach key lessons to younger children: the value of time and the skill of being able to relax by changing activity rather than by just wasting time or doing nothing:

- Agree on a getting up time of say 7.30 am or 8 am. Otherwise much of the self-discipline from term time is undermined.
- Promote new hobbies, build communication and presentation skills, foster a love of art, drama or music. Help your child grow intellectually, physically, culturally, and in qualities of character.
- Don't let closed-mindedness enter your house. Take a lively interest in the rest of the world. Lead by example. Together, do acts of service for others.
- Put aside a little time each day for each child to spend on a job around home.
- Don't take the default option of letting inane television programs babysit your children. Avoid soaps and sitcoms which tell us nothing new. Watch interesting movies and documentaries. Talk about them.
- Let your children see you reading. One mum sets aside a half-hour each morning in the holidays during which everyone in the house reads. It works.

2 Delegate, even if it takes more time to get the job done

'Mum shouldn't do anything anyone else can do, and if no-one else can do it, then teach 'em how.'

First Corollary to the Law of Domestic Expectations

Children take so long to do things. No wonder parents end up doing so much for their children – cleaning up after them, picking up after them, making their beds. It can seem more efficient *not* to delegate, and it is certainly a lot less trouble. But this is short-term thinking.

Initial training takes time, but later on the economies come. Get the kids involved when they're young and want to help, even if it takes more time to do the job. And, as a bonus, they will continue helping when they are older, when they are much more useful.

In larger families delegation is a must to survive, but in all families it is the key to developing a sense of responsibility in kids. Rosters and planning out jobs for even the smallest kids will pay big dividends when teenage years arrive. Take the initiative: plan responsibilities for all the members of the family with your spouse or in a family discussion. Help children to set their own goals, and frequently review them.

Objective goals can help to make jobs and responsibilities clearer and make each child more accountable. Facts speak for themselves and allow your reprimands or praise to be more educationally effective. One parent's policy: 'Kids respect what we inspect.' Another espouses a variation: 'It's not what we expect, it's what we inspect.' Close follow-up of jobs and duties given to children is *absolutely* essential if we are to build good habits.

Responsibilities don't need to be big. A child who grows up with a sense of responsibility in small things will be responsible in big things later on.

Possible jobs for a seven-year-old child

Insist that regular jobs should be done without being asked. Expect a consciousness of time. Insist even on some jobs the child may not like. Teach simple responsibilities for hygiene. Create a culture where we help each other.

Care of clothing

- Ensure that what goes to school comes home.
- Hang up their clothing and polish their own shoes.
- Place dirty clothes in the washing basket.

Room

- Make bed on getting up.
- Tidy room. Put toys put away in organiser boxes.

School belongings

- Pack their own bag and remember special activities for next day, i.e. sport/library/music.
- Make own list of things to remember for each day of the week.
- Make and pack own lunch.
- Unpack lunchbox and hand over any notes from school.

Inside jobs

- Get up when first called.
- Clean wash basin.
- Answer telephone courteously.
- Encourage some responsibility for younger brothers and sisters, e.g. changing the baby's nappy, bathing a younger child.
- Simple cooking, even having a weekly night to help cook.
- Unpack a part of the dishwasher. Set table and clean away. Sweep the kitchen floor. Take out kitchen tidy at the end of the day. Bring in the bin.
- Do a weekend job out of a *job jar*. Vacuum the bedrooms. Clean windows.
- Put washing/ironing away.
- Feed animals and make sure the bowls are clean.
- Write their own party invitations.

Outside

- Carry out a specific task in the garden before play.
- Pick up sticks, help with weeding, take leaves out of the pool.
- Help to wash the car. Vacuum the inside.
- Simple shopping. Check change.

Timetable and homework

- Keep to a standard routine with few variations.
- Keep to a schedule on a whiteboard.
- Expect simple and reasonable goals on holidays/weekends.
- Keep to a nightly routine of learning spelling, reading and tables. This will be a foundation for good study habits in later years.
- If an instrument is being learnt, maintain a routine of nightly music practice.

3 Teach that actions should be motivated by love

'Through virtues we deliver love to others.'

DR DONALD DEMARCO, CANADIAN PHILOSOPHER

Your family is the *ideal* environment for fostering good habits. Service to others is the lynchpin of harmonious family life. The natural motive for actions in a family is love. In a family we are accepted because we are a member of that family, because of *who we are*, not because of *what we do*. All children are treated equally, with all the affection and attention they need to become the best they each can be. Only personal love can discover the individualised goals each individual character requires.

Dr Donald DeMarco explains that strengths of character empower us to love others effectively. His *Heart of Virtue* is a collection of wonderful stories to illustrate virtues. The title alludes to the loving intention at the heart of every good habit. It is no good being a sensitive communicator who is faithless to his wife or partner, nor a teenager with all the appearances of politeness who does what he or she likes away from home.

Caritas

Underpinning every good habit must be a loving intention. Augustine said that *caritas*, charity, contains all the cardinal virtues. By this he meant, for example, that fortitude requires a noble, loving intention. The brazenness of a successful bankrobber is actually a vice for it is motivated by an evil intention. Similarly, if a person donates large amounts to charity in order to be noticed by others, neither responsibility nor justice are present. To swindle the tax department is not sound judgement.

Unconditional parental love – love that never gets fed up – is the vital model for a child's future spousal love. It may mean the difference between a relationship that weathers the storms and one that gets washed away. But never think that unconditional love means never correcting children. Rather, corrections must be motivated by love.

Love for a child does not depend on what they do, or don't, achieve

You must be proud of your son?' a journalist asked the mother of Johnnie Wilkinson, player of the 2003 Rugby World Cup.

Johnnie's mum replied, 'I'm proud of all *my children.'*

Either we imbue a child's upbringing with a deep love for others, or the default setting is selfishness. For this reason, there is no such thing as value-free education. Hence institutions must assist in fostering character: respect for others; healthy expectations of putting one's talents at the service of others; exposure to positive role-models; a positive philosophy of education where mistakes are part of the process of learning, where problems are not seen as disasters but rather as opportunities to address an underlying cause that is now in the open. But because institutions tend to treat education as a mass production process their effectiveness only extends so far.

Tapping into timeless wisdom

The teachings of Confucius may be summed up in one word, *jen*, meaning love, humanity, goodness, benevolence. He taught:

'Virtue is to love men. Wisdom is to understand men.'

It is no surprise to see in the greatest pagan philosophers of ancient Rome a virtually identical exhortation to universal love for one's fellow man. Cicero wrote:

'Virtue joins man to God: all human beings have an inherent worth, the universal brotherhood of man.'

Foster a loving intention

'Do this to help mum' is one of the most powerful lines a father can use. And mum can whisper in the ear of her seven-year-old, 'You know how much dad loves you to do your reading'.

Parents who use the big stick approach, 'Do this because I said so', set themselves up for a fall when their children are teenagers. Rather, we should consistently teach children to act out of love for those around them.

4 Don't let bad habits accumulate

'It is the worst impressions on a young person that are most durable.'

QUINTILIAN, 35 – c. 100

The children of some parents can do no wrong. Teachers are all too aware how quickly some parents fly to the defence of their children. How many excuses we can have for our children's behaviour ... and for our own mistakes as well!

We need objective eyes to look at our children. Too often we look on fondly as bad habits develop. We are fooling ourselves when we say, 'They'll grow out of it'; we let the child down.

> *'A young person's character is like wax for the growth of bad habits.'*
>
> HORACE, 65–8 BC

Just as deeply rooted habitual good actions motivated by loving intention are virtues, bad habits or actions with selfish motivation are vices. Habits, by their very nature, are meant to be permanent, so let us keep our focus on building up good habits in children and fight like there is no tomorrow to prevent the build-up of vices in their character.

Vices are similarly fostered by repeated actions. So a boy who *repeatedly* dodges homework develops an entrenched irresponsibility; *repeatedly* teasing others will create a habit whereby the person becomes hardened to the difficulties of others.

Vices can cramp a child's potential for life. It is important to follow up and correct bad behaviour *before* it becomes entrenched as a bad habit. We ignore this warning at our children's peril. How many children later lose marriages or jobs because their parents were ineffective in teaching that young person to master incipient bad behaviours.

Correct children firmly but calmly. Give reasons to the head, and affection to the heart. Are your corrections positive? Is there overreliance on reprimands and deprivations?

Do you teach your child to show love in his or her deeds? Do you allow children to redeem themselves?

> *'Listen to what your child has to say: allow time to check your emotion, and allow reason to find what punishment is appropriate.'*
>
> PLUTARCH, 46–120

Negative behaviours do not come from a vacuum. Child psychologist Michele Borba says, 'The best way to stop an inappropriate behaviour is by getting at the root of the problem – what's causing it in the first place.' The next time you get annoyed with your children, ask yourself where they learnt the behaviour. Either they learnt it at home, ultimately from you, or they learnt it from peer or media influences. Neither option is very flattering. You are either giving a poor example yourself or, if they brought the behaviour home, it means that your own parenting is on the weak side, unable to outweigh the negative example of others. Are you in the game?

> *Finally the television is turned off after yet another battle of wills. Carly explains to her mother, 'You wouldn't have to go through this if you'd just do what I tell you.'*

Manage negative habit-forming activities

Certain behaviours are habit forming by their very repetitive and appealing nature:

- excessive TV and computer time
- curiosity on the Internet
- snacking at will
- talking negatively of others
- ducking out of jobs
- 'forgetting'
- letting someone else do it or take over
- quitting when jobs are tough
- telling half-truths
- obsessive collecting.

If such behaviours are not particularly good for children, parents need to read the play quickly. Some regulatory guidelines may be called for.

5 Don't do the thinking for your child

'The best managers know how to manage themselves.'

PETER DRUCKER, GURU OF MANAGEMENT THEORY

Control your hyperparent gene. Do not overmanage your child. If you do not raise children to manage themselves, they will be ineffective in life. Keep checking for the 'learned helplessness' that Martin Seligman first spotted on the radar screen. These are the things that children need to be taught:

1 **Teach goal-setting.** When the school report comes home, 'sit on the same side of the table', as Rafael Pich says, with your son or daughter. Help them look objectively at the good and the bad. Help them to formulate a couple of resolutions for the coming term. Then show them that goals without monitoring usually don't work.

2 **Teach problem-solving.** Help your son or daughter identify the objective issues, and form appropriate strategies.

3 **Teach your child about emotions and passions**. Emphasise reason over impulsive reactions: 'Don't rush in. Think about it!' Teach them various strategies to manage their emotional reactions: taking time out, delaying decisions, talking themselves into calming down, deciding beforehand on the battles they will fight, etc.

4 **Help children draw up their own simple personal timetables** – not the unrealistic, draconian sort we have all failed to keep at times. Take your older and younger children shopping and let them choose the diary and the wall planner for their schoolwork.

5 **Encourage them to plan out their holidays and social activities.** Don't organise parties *for* them; help them organise them *for themselves*. Be supportive; channel, don't stifle. Be involved from the start, but don't take over. Help them see that inexperience can lead to problems, and that your only concern is their welfare.

6 **Consult your children for their opinions.** Have round-table discussions. We all need to feel we have been listened to.

7 **Let them make up their own minds** when there is no risk of moral or physical danger. Then debrief afterwards. If your fourteen-year-old son wants to stay home and study when the rest of the family goes to Gran's, let him, and talk afterwards about Granny sending her love. Drop him over the next week after his exams. You will win much more this way – you will win your child's heart.

The Imperial game plan

The Emperor Augustus asked a great deal of his adopted sons: 'When they were still young, he gave them political responsibility, and sent them out to command provinces and armies …', a contemporary biographer writes. He realised that if those young people were to be leaders they needed to learn those skills earlier rather than later.

How are your goals?

Give children experience in setting their own goals and guide them through the process. It does help, though, to be on the same wavelength. One teacher was talking to a student: 'John, we talked about goals last week. How was your goal this week?'

'You should have seen it, Sir, I kicked it with my left foot.'

You can take a horse to water …

In an effort to walk one young man through the need to set appropriate goals for himself in personal presentation, his mum put him in front of a mirror. His tie was askew, his shirt pocket torn, his shirt filthy and his hair chaotic: 'Christopher, look and tell me, what's wrong?' Christopher looks and says cautiously, 'My socks are down?' True story!

Teach healthy self-reflection

'Everyone should say, "Where did I go wrong? What duty was not done?"'

PLUTARCH, 46–120

6 Model the qualities you want to pass on

'The children of drunkards cannot be expected to walk straight in mind or in body.'

Plato, 428–348 BC

Homer Simpson will have more influence on your child than you do if Homer spends more time with your son. Children will imitate anyone or anything they spend time with. Don't rationalise your way around it. Children need the maximal personal attention from both mum and dad.

At my school we regularly run father–son camps. These weekends bring fathers closer to their children, the dads learn by watching other dads in action, and they grow in friendship with each other. How similar dads and their sons are! Boys copy their fathers in most things – in their way of walking and laughing, in the sports they like, in the way they tease others, even in how they wear a baseball cap.

A role model even in this!

Gus is a particularly fussy ten-year-old. His fussiness extends to not eating his lunch. The food he most despises, understandably some might say, is the egg-plant sandwiches his mother often gives him. Regularly he arrives home without his lunch eaten, expecting to receive a large, delicious afternoon tea of his favourite things. Often his self-imposed hunger would be appeased prior to reaching home for he would convince his mother to stop at KFC.

Mum was not surprised that her son was so fussy. 'When we go out to a barbecue his father always refuses to eat. He waits until we reach home because he prefers my cooking.'

Later, discussing the possible reasons that Gus does not use the school toilets, Dad speaks up, 'When I'm at work, I always hold on until I get home!'

Aristotle's familiar saying, 'The child is father of the man', reminds us that we cannot underestimate the importance of those first habit-forming years. In the character of the child the adult may already be discerned. Everything we say and do leaves an impression. And remember, it is very natural for your child to put you on a pedestal until he or she is about thirteen. Use this time to maximise your example, not to draw maximum adulation. Try not to be in it for yourself.

When a child grows up in a home where adults don't apologise, where the tone of conversation is sarcastic or negative, where there is little apparent affection, where there is a poor spirit of service to the others in the home, where people eat whenever, whatever or however much they like, where television is more interesting than each other's company, or where there is no example of industriousness, that child will labour under these encumbrances throughout life, and perhaps visit them on their own children in turn.

Bottom lines for parents

- Scrupulously avoid arguing in front of your child or children.
- Strive to model constant affection and self-sacrifice.
- Avoid bad language, crass jokes, violence and objectionable material on television.
- Don't leave it up to others to provide stimulation for your child.
- Don't be sarcastic or critical of persons who are not present.
- Don't talk more enthusiastically about self-centred activities than about service to others.
- Surround your children with hope and idealism.

It's in the way you say it

We don't say, 'We can't afford that,' with glum faces. Rather, to teach our children to spend on needs, not wants, we say to them in an upbeat way, 'We're not going to spend money on that!'

David and Marie

Think about it!

'Dad, why are you cooking?'
'It's Mother's Day.'
'So is every other day Father's Day?'

7 Clearly teach what is right and wrong

'I know the difference between right and wrong. I am no longer a child.'

SON OF ODYSSEUS, PROCLAIMING HIS MATURITY

The capacity to distinguish right from wrong is a key feature of a maturing character. Homer saw it as the defining marker of adulthood.

Adults in the making need a clear *understanding of the objective reasons* for doing the right thing – reasons based first of all on love for others, for the good of their own health and happiness, and on a shared responsibility to make this world a more human place in the deepest sense of the word.

And they need abundant *practice in discernment*. What we practise, we master – we become truly discerning. This capacity to distinguish is what mankind for centuries has called conscience. For Stephen Covey, *conscience* is not religious jargon, but one of the four great gifts of human nature, along with self-awareness, an independent will, and imagination. All four gifts must be developed, he says. Three out of four mean failure: Vlad the Impaler had three in abundance, particularly imagination it would seem, but he had no conscience, and hence was a dismal failure as a human being.

Don't patronise your children. Give real reasons; don't just shoot from the hip. Think through the best reasons for living a good life and doing good for others. Use the dinnertable for discussion, but first do your homework; come prepared with spot-on explanations. Sit together and talk about television programs and videos. Let your child see you take action when something is not good enough. Turn off the TV and write to the station if the program becomes offensive.

No-one else has the right to set the moral agenda for your child – not a teacher, not a politician, not the local librarian, and certainly not a gutter-mouthed disc jockey. No question we should avoid burdening an impressionable child with a raft of arbitrary parental opinions, but it is a parent's solemn duty to teach the knowledge that can mean the difference between life and death, between happiness and a life sentenced to self-centred bitterness. In today's drug and alcohol youth culture this is so true. Statistically your child will be deeply disappointed in a failed relationship. You can do something to alter this outcome.

> *'Try not to become a person of success, but a person of value.'*
>
> ALBERT EINSTEIN, 1879–1955

Go easy on the rules

If pre-teen children do not learn that love must underpin their actions, they will think that right is defined by rules – and you will have a devil of a time trying to find rules for every possible misbehaviour. The sense of right and wrong must be *interiorly* adopted, not just *exteriorly* imposed.

Cato's advice for his son

Cato the Elder (d. 149 BC), the greatest Roman of his times, left a collection of sayings for his son. It represents the effort of a conscientious parent to pass on to his child clear and unambiguous guidelines for a good life. In them, many parents will recognise their own words to their children: 'Pray to God', 'Love your parents', 'Keep company of good people', and 'Don't drink too much'. And two particularly applicable to today's primary students: 'Keep what is given to you' and 'Read books'.

Other rules are perhaps less spoken of today, and perhaps therefore all the more missed. 'Preserve modesty', advice that is better imparted before teenage egos are involved. 'Don't sneer at the poor' nags at our developed world consciences. 'Greet freely' refers to the disappearing art of making others feel welcome. 'Don't laugh at anybody' is good advice for our own dinnertables. And 'Study literature' is a timeless antidote to the XBox.

Of all the 57 sayings, two are my favourites: *Parentem parientem vince* ('Overcome your parent with patience'). What a wonderful recipe to avoid arguments! And *Convivare raro* ('Don't party too much'). Good advice to kids in any civilisation.

8 Help your children build good habits in their younger years

'Anything a child receives into his mind is likely to become indelible and unalterable.'

Plato, 428–348 BC

Early childhood studies are showing how important early experience is in children's learning. Elementary neuronal networks in the brain require stimulation from the external environment for consolidation. After about ten years of age, the brain preserves only those pathways that have been reinforced through experience; the rest it destroys. This is a physiological explanation for why an ear for languages or music is best acquired at an early age. Neurologists say that it is *repeated* experience that wires a child's brain. This is a physiological explanation for the importance of routines and good habits.

Of course this works in reverse. A child with the habit of eating whenever he wants is wired for problems in later life. The habits acquired in early years for better or for worse seem to endure – the openness or the lack of trust, the tendency to face or avoid the truth, the industriousness or the laziness, the generosity or the selfishness, the habit of reflection or the rashness, the kindness or the insensitivity. A child who has a television dependency when five years of age will lack willpower in front of a video screen during teen years, when his parents would rather he studied. As James Stenson wryly says, 'Pay now or pay later, but either way you pay'. Win those battles of establishing routines and behaviours now, otherwise there will be angst all round come adolescence.

Children who don't play much, or are rarely touched, develop brains 20 percent to 30 percent smaller than normal for their age.

Research results from Baylor College of Medicine

Windows of opportunity

There are *windows* in the life of a child when certain habits are best learnt. Later it is much harder. For example, if eight-year-olds don't learn to put work before play, they will make heavy going of their studies through secondary school. They may even be groping for the necessary industriousness and internal motivation throughout tertiary years.

Fortunately there is a back door. By a great act of the will we can acquire behaviours after that optimal window has shut. But it means a lot of extra work, and can imply some fairly average parenting along the way.

Let's do our children the great favour of presenting them with the right challenges (and the right example) at the appropriate time. What a pity when a child, already a teenager, is still struggling with self-control or respect for others.

Discover ways to pattern your small child's behaviour

Look for consistency of parental example, orderly routines and clear expectations of responsibility:

- Look at home culture. Look at the culture in your child's classroom. Look at the culture in the sporting team. Manage the inputs your child is receiving.
- Look at ways to focus on repeated actions – giving a particular job to a child, having a particular time each day when a particular job is done, etc.
- Look at your habitual ways of talking and acting; these will become the habitual ways of talking and acting of your child.
- Foster a deep and abiding love for the good, the true, and the beautiful, remembering that children always like best those things they first experience.
- Underpin all your parental example with a deep respect and compassion for others. It will rub off.

Teacher to seven-year-old: 'Do you make your bed?'
'Yes.' (Nodding solemnly)
'How often?'
'Once a fortnight.'

9 Make character building the aim of children's sport

'Laziness is the habit of resting before fatigue sets in.'

Jack Gibson, a founder of modern Rugby League

One parent recently told me that she drove in and out of home twelve times by noon on a Saturday ferrying her children to and from sport. Why go to such effort providing children's sport? What are the aims of children's sport? Why are we investing so much capital in fields and pools and gyms?

Besides its potential for sheer enjoyment, sport is a feature of sound health education for children. We all have heard the alarming statistics about increasing obesity in children. Sport also provides a terrific opportunity for parents to spend time with their sons and daughters. But surely the greatest benefit of sport lies in its potential for character development.

Sport is ideal for building habits. The very enjoyable nature of sport makes sporting experiences so vivid. And the routines of sport lend themselves to the repeated experiences upon which good habits *can* be built. The frequent practising, the team culture, the demands of a game, and even the disappointments of missing selection, can drill fortitude and mental resilience. But without the right guidance, team culture can just as easily reinforce habits of lack of respect for others, vanity and thuggery.

Remember the film *Hoosiers*? The coach and manager of children's teams have the privileged opportunity of leaving a lasting legacy – as long as they remember that their players will particularly imitate those adults who take an interest in them. If they think the aim of children's sport is winning above all, they may well be effective coaches, but dismal failures as mentors. What a pity!

Children imitate the behaviour around them, and therefore the coach needs, at all times, to communicate respect for others, realising that a deep respect for others is the most essential of all personality traits. Example in this must never be compromised. The coach and manager must model self-control. They must strive to correct mistakes calmly, never berating, never belittling in public, making all criticism constructive, and looking forward, never back, to harp on mistakes.

Professionalism in coaching is so important, and fortunately there are now outstanding role models in this regard from professional sport. When the coach is well prepared and punctual, and teaches each individual in the team to strive for his or her personal best effort through personal goals, then we are really talking character building.

A coach must never think less of a team member simply because that player is less capable than the star player in the team. In life the bar is not at the same height for every person – we all have differing talents. A player does not deserve more respect because he has scored the points, nor less, because he has missed a tackle.

What a mistake when we adults put too much emphasis on winning. In one particular age group in my school the soccer and the rugby teams were enjoying very different fortunes. One team trounced every opponent. The other team suffered the longest of seasons, but they continued to be commended for their rousing three cheers for the opposition teams that were thrashing them week after week. Who could claim that the boys in the winning team grew more in character that season than those in the losing team? In fact the winners were notoriously slack trainers and became a little arrogant with all their successes. Be convinced that there is as much potential for building character in losing as in winning.

Never underestimate strength of character

'What will they send me next?'

PE TEACHER'S WORDS ON FIRST SIGHT OF A GANGLY AND SCRAWNY EDMUND HILLARY ENTERING HIS CLASS IN SECONDARY SCHOOL

Classic tips about children's sport

Parents must not be in it for themselves:
'Having lost our agility, we delight in their sports and merrymaking, because we love to think of our former selves. We gladly institute contests for those who are able to awaken in us the memory of our youth.'

PLATO, 428–348 BC

Keep sport in perspective:
'Parents who devote their children to gymnastics while they neglect their necessary education, in reality vulgarise them.'

ARISTOTLE, 384–322 BC

Bad habits creep into sport as well:
'In competing with boys his own age, he should neither be allowed to give up nor to lose his temper.'

SENECA, 4 BC – 65 AD

Provide physical challenges

We do no favour to children when we make life as easy as possible. Cato, the most famous Roman of his time, himself taught his son 'gymnastic exercises, how to throw a dart, fight in armour, ride, box, endure both heat and cold and to swim the most rapid and rough rivers'.

Do you go on bushwalks and push yourself physically in your parenting. When was the last time you said, 'Let's walk there', or 'Give me a hand to do this out in the garden'?

Lead from the front: choose to get up early more often, keep fit, avoid the slightest symptoms of feeling sorry for yourself.

How hard do you push – literally?

When she was about eleven years old, we took our eldest daughter, who had already learnt to swim, to the pool for squads. She refused to get in the water, probably embarrassed. She was gently told that she could get in on her own or be helped by her parents, fully clothed. She did get into the water that day. Years later, she would represent her school at swimming carnivals and wind up teaching learn-to-swim classes at that very same swim school.

ANNE, MOTHER OF SEVEN

10 Show your children that hard lessons can be the best lessons

'If a child has always been given everything he asked for, if his anxious mother always comforted him when he cried, if his child minder always let him do what he wanted, then he will never be able to cope with anything unpleasant in life.'

SENECA, 4 BC – 65 AD

Earlier we looked at the kindness that debilitates children, and at the importance of having a child accept the consequences of his or her actions. Here we turn to the importance of a degree of physical demand on children.

No, we do not need to be Spartans who washed babies in wine instead of water to toughen them up! But surely there is some middle ground between thickshakes every afternoon and the ancient practice of putting all the village children into a common eating hall. And while Spartan children wore but a single garment all year round, there must be a healthier alternative to stocking up on expensive designer brands.

To the Spartans' credit 'they trained children to eat up their food and not to be fussy about it, not to be frightened of the dark, or of being left alone, and not to be prone to ill-bred fits of temper or crying'. Such a reputation did the Spartan women have for raising resilient children that they worked in other parts of Greece as *au pairs* and contract nannies.

In every age, there are parents who have spoilt their children to the lasting unhappiness of the children. Cicero writes about his spoiled nephew: 'He has always been indulged by his father … making him headstrong, overbearing and aggressive'. He recognised that an indulged child will have little self-control, even in matters of controlling his own temper, impatience or wilfulness. A dangerous cocktail!

> *'Do not spoil them and do not physic them, that about sums it up.'*
>
> JOHN KNIGHTLY ON RAISING CHILDREN, JANE AUSTEN, *EMMA*

Be demanding

'Be demanding. This is positive advice. Many people equate being demanding with taking away the children's freedom … However freedom only exists if a person is able to make a choice. A person who cannot read has no freedom because of his inability to read. The person who can read is free to choose which book to read, even whether to read or not …'

MARGARET AND GERARD O'DONNELL, *FAMILY VALUES*

Parental perseverance

When we wanted Mark, our nine-year-old, to start making his bed, we gave what we thought were good reasons like it's good to be neat and orderly, and you should take responsibility for your room. Mark explained, rather inevitably, that he didn't mind if his bed wasn't made, and so he wouldn't make it. We said we wanted it made; so he said that it was his bed and he was happy to sleep in it unmade! I wanted the house to be neat, so Mark offered to shut his door! We then said, 'Just make it!' A few days later Mark asked if he could sleep in his sleeping bag for fun, and I, unsuspecting, said yes. For weeks Mark then slept in the sleeping bag laid out on the already made bed. Eventually the arrangement was becoming so unhygienic we insisted that he hang the bag on the line as it was. About this time Mark discovered he could slide into bed without disturbing the sheets and slide out again in the morning. This then went on for some time until finally, I'm pleased to say, through common sense and fine reasoning, we wore him down. Mark now makes his bed – but it was touch and go there for a while.

GAI AND GREGORY

Radical consequences

'My father used to take the television to the tip regularly.'

JULES, 33 YEARS OF AGE

'Once dad got so cranky that we wouldn't turn off the tele that he got out the pliers and cut the cord. It was okay for him, he and mum had another TV in their bedroom!

MATTIE, 30 YEARS OF AGE.

11 Keep focused on sincerity and generosity – habits for our heads and our hearts

'It is natural for the mind to believe, and for the will to love; so that, for want of true objects, they must attach themselves to the false.'

BLAISE PASCAL, 1623–1662

Knowing and loving are the natural functions of the human mind and will. These activities need to be underpinned by strong habits of sincerity and generosity.

Sincerity is the habit proper to the intellect. Sincerity is essential if we are to be able to seek and recognise the truth about ourselves and about others, and if we are to be able to face objectively the impact of our actions on others, if we are to be direct and transparent in relationships and face up to the duties permanent relationships place on us.

'Nature has instilled in our minds an insatiable desire to see truth.'

CICERO, 106–43 BC

Sincerity

The word 'sincerity' is supposed to have come from the Latin *sine* (without) plus *cera* (wax). Two theories account for this. One holds that sculptors sought out blocks of marble which were flawless, undoctored by unscrupulous quarry owners who would try to sell blocks having imperfections plugged with wax. Another theory states that when a messenger was totally trustworthy his master would entrust to him messages which were not sealed with wax. In both honesty is demonstrated.

Generosity perfects the will, enriches us with a deeply compassionate and respectful spirit, orients us towards relationships, and ultimately, empowers us to love. Professor David Isaacs says, 'Generous people act unselfishly and cheerfully for the benefit of others, conscious of the value of their help and despite the fact that it may cost them an effort'. Generosity is a necessary pathway to discovering the self-giving love that gives the most certain meaning to life.

Generosity

Generosity is the proper habit of the human capacity of choice, our will. If freedom does not lead eventually to love it has been squandered. Every choice we make is either egocentric, or us/other-centred. Habitually self-centred choices strangle relationships. Perhaps for this reason we talk metaphorically of the will as the *heart* of a human being, the seat of love and of choice.

Think of sincerity and generosity as the software that runs on our human operating system. A perennial bedrock axiom about human beings is that they can only be satisfied by truth and love. Without sincerity and generosity a child will be incapable of knowing reality, and incapable of giving himself or herself to others in love. How many children do we see in denial about problems, fudging the truth, and failing to open themselves to responsibility for others? But how many adults can confidently say they are totally honest with themselves and with others, and that they always put those who are closest to them before themselves? This is no small problem.

'A first-class brain and a second-class will always will be defeated by a second-class brain and a first-class will.'

Jack Gibson, a founder of modern Rugby League

'Where there's a will there's a solicitor.'

Answer on a Year 6 test

The link between sincerity and generosity – between self-knowledge and self-giving

'Self-knowledge leads to self-mastery. Self-mastery leads to self-giving, the foundation for loving relationships.'

Professor David Isaacs, University of Navarre

Teaching sincerity

'He hath ever but slenderly known himself.'

SHAKESPEARE, *KING LEAR*

As sincerity is a necessity in adult life it must be established as a habit in a young person. It is not normal for children to be insincere. Insincerity in children may be caused by fear, by peer example, by an ingrained habit from early childhood, by the desire to impress, or by parent example, but whatever the cause, it needs to be addressed. A seven or eight year old should know the difference between fact and fancy. Some parents notice that their children go through a stage where they seem to lie. While understanding this, we should insist on the truth, but be sensitive to the *possibility* that the child's suspected lying is really a product of forgetfulness or dreaming.

The following methods of ensuring that your child grows to be truthful and sincere are drawn from the collective wisdom of many parents:

1 Model integrity. Accept feedback humbly and make resolutions to fix whatever needs fixing. Let children see your own efforts to improve, particularly in your work, and by hearing you apologise after life's inevitable mistakes.

2 Help your child to have an objective view of their *own* many qualities and of areas where they need to improve.

3 Trust your child's word, unless the evidence is irrefutable.

4 Correct each small act of insincerity. Don't let opportunities pass to teach this vital virtue. It is too important. Show affection – you are correcting out of love. Help your son or daughter to see that your only goal is their welfare.

5 Allow natural consequences to take their course – a lie to a teacher should be fixed by honesty and an apology, shoplifting requires restitution and face-to-face apology, etc. Explain your reasons for insisting on consequences.

6 Show your child that insincerity harms others and between adults can break trust virtually irreparably. Agree on a concrete plan to fix things up. And then firmly, but with infinite affection, hold your child to the agreement.

7 Defer meting out punishments while you are emotional. 'In a heated argument we are apt to lose sight of the truth', taught Publilius Syrus in the first century BC. It is good if parents also help each other in this.

8 If you have become angry, apologise for the harsh things *you* said and make sure you listen to your child's view.

9 When making a point to an older child, use David Isaacs's 3Cs. Be *clear*, be *concise*, and then *change* the subject.

10 Help your child to internalise the lesson by reflecting on the causes and consequences of their actions.

To what age do you accept tall stories?

About the time when Harry Potter first started talking to snakes, a seven-year-old told me that he had seen a snake the previous weekend – 'a yellow-bellied black snake ... from here to the door [a healthy length by any serpentine standards – about four metres]. I killed it with my pocket knife.' With my eyebrows raised I rang his mother. 'Have you had some trouble with snakes recently?' The story was pure fabrication.

Teaching honesty and openness to a seven-year-old child

- Remind your child that you were seven once, so you know a story when you hear one.
- Make eye contact – it makes it more difficult for a child to lie.
- To help your child never be afraid of telling the truth because of the punishment, ask 'What do you think is a fair punishment?'
- Don't punish for telling the truth about a wrongdoing and give praise for having the courage to tell the truth, to give the child a way out.
- Teach the importance of deep contrition for mistakes, as we can only correct mistakes we have acknowledged in our hearts.

Testimonies to sincerity

'Know thyself' INSCRIBED OVER THE CAVE ENTRANCE TO THE ORACLE OF DELPHI

'Sincerity and truth are the basis of every virtue.' CONFUCIUS, 551–479 BC

'The unexamined life is not worth living.' SOCRATES, 469–399 BC

'Do not pretend one thing and do another.' CICERO, 106–43 BC

'If you add to the truth, you subtract from it.' THE TALMUD

'Don't wear different faces in different places.' A TIMELESS CATALAN SAYING

Creating a culture of generosity in the home

'It is not the brains that matter most, but that which guides them – the character, the heart, generous qualities …'

FYODOR MIKHAYLOVICH DOSTOYEVSKY, 1821–1881

Consider the old adage: 'A good person loves people and uses things, while a bad person loves things and uses people'. Do you live for others? Or are things a little back to front?

Be aware that the secret ingredient of loving relationships is unconditional service.

This idea came through so clearly at a wedding of friends. The celebrant said with great affection, 'It's a matter of giving until you don't know if there will be anything left for yourself!' Maybe some marriages fail because one of the partners gets tired of giving, but perhaps more come apart because such dedication isn't promised at the start, nor discussed openly when the air pockets start to toss the couple around. We all begin new endeavours idealistically and generously; marriage is no exception. But if we set our sights too low, old habits will come back to haunt us. Initial emotions of love help us to give of ourselves completely; but if we are not living for each other by the time the first fires burn down it can all seem too difficult.

Model the nothing's-a-problem attitude as this will help your children so much in their lives ahead. Don't allow a culture of complaining to take root in your home. And that means never catch yourself complaining – about anything – even under your breath, even in your mind! That is hard.

> *'Worry comes with wealth;*
> *Our thirst for more grows*
> *As our fortunes grow.'*
> HORACE 65–8 BC

The 80–20 rule

James Stenson coined the 80–20 rule. He insists that both partners in a marriage should set out to give 80 percent and expect only 20 percent back; in other words, not to keep a book on who is doing more, but to positively set out to give as much as possible. In one of his lectures, one mischievous voice interrupted, 'I walk out the door in the morning. My wife says goodbye to me and she thinks she's done her 80 percent!' His wife was beside him laughing and laughing.

A feature of a culture of generosity in the home is that parents place a high value on friendships, and on teaching children the qualities of friendship.

'What is a friend?' Aristotle asked two and a half thousand years ago. He answered, 'A single soul dwelling in two bodies'. Without giving of oneself, a human being is isolated. He or she will move through life like a rock in space, but with no possibility of happiness, only short-lived pleasures. We cannot condemn children to this. Friendship teaches this quality. Unfortunately children will find it hard to make real friendships if they do not see that their parents have numerous friends, whose joys and sorrows they readily speak of.

So don't forget to involve children when guests are over. Expect them to show courtesy by giving their full attention, turning off the television, staying at the table during the whole meal, farewelling politely, and so on. Encourage children, too, in their own friendships by having their friends over and by giving them ideas on how to help their friends.

A sad tale of friendlessness

I will never forget a very distressing parent/teacher interview years ago. The mother of a pretty but withdrawn Year 7 girl told me, 'I tell Ophelia not to have friends, they only let you down.' Ophelia had been raised to mistrust everyone. No doubt somewhere in the past mum had been badly let down, but what a tragic message to give any child!

The direct approach

'I wish I didn't have any sisters', one girl tells her father.

'That's exactly why you need them, so that you grow up not to be rotten and selfish' was the quick reply.

'A good heart these days is hard to find.'

Stevie Nicks

Fostering solidarity with those who are less fortunate

'I don't know what your destiny will be, but one thing I know; the only ones among you who will be really happy are those who will have sought and found how to serve.'

Albert Schweitzer, 1875–1965

F Scott Fitzgerald quipped, 'The world as a rule does not live on beaches and in country clubs'. It is calculated that the resources of the 13 richest families in the world would feed the world's poor for the next 50 years. A recent UN report stated that 25 percent of Africans are undernourished. One billion people live in slums in the world and the same number live on less than $1 a day. Twenty-six thousand Australian teenagers live on the street. Yet despite all this, many of our children remain insulated from the pressing needs of other human beings. Two thousand years ago Seneca appealed, 'Attend to any poor wretch as your fellow man'; one thousand years ago the Chinese scholar, Chang Tsai, proclaimed, 'All people are my brothers and sisters'. But are we listening?

There is more happiness in giving than in receiving, yet even our politicians are justifying international policy on the basis of national self-interest! And Oxfam is finding that the developed world is only giving half the aid it was twenty years ago to the Third World, as a percentage of GDP.

Children cannot do much about poverty in the developing world, but if they are to do anything about it in their adult lives, they must develop well-oiled habits of generosity and solidarity with those less fortunate when they are young. For them to do so primarily depends on the attitudes they see lived out at home. But ACER research gives some cause for concern that positive civic attitudes are not being effectively fostered in Australian children.

Practical idealism

One family had the simple custom of lighting a candle on the hallway table to remind them to pray for a friend or relative who had died. The son who grew up in that home is now an officer of the law, and the daughter who worked as a lay missionary for two years is now the Rwandan coordinator for a major aid organisation. Don't underestimate small family customs in building a culture of solidarity.

Mother Teresa's words should not be an indictment of our own homes: 'The less one has the more one gives'. Let's teach generosity by our own example – giving money to good causes, sharing things, doing jobs for elderly relatives. With King Lear we all have cause to say, 'I have taken too little care of this!', when we see the needs of others. We need to give children's natural idealism an outlet. Two parents I know are helping their children raise money so that they can participate in a community service project in Fiji. Often all young people need is our know-how and encouragement.

Throw yourself into idealistic causes, and talk about them at home with passion. I have seen the great good that comes when families talk about ideals around the dinner table.

'There is no greater satisfaction for a just and well-meaning person than the knowledge that he has devoted his best energies to the service of a good cause.'

ALBERT EINSTEIN, 1879–1955

Just do it!

One dad wanted to teach compassion to his fifteen-year-old son. The boy was badgering him to buy him yet another pair of $200 Nikes. His father said, 'Come on mate, let's go out for dinner'. He took him into the city and they stood together in the queue of a city soup kitchen. Now, two years later, one night each week the son helps run the soup kitchen!

Generosity solves many teenage problems

Professor David Isaacs insists that 'Your child must experience the joy that comes from serving others'. He says the antidote to the introspection and self-centredness that can take over in teenage years is education in generosity.

We must nourish the idealism of teenagers. Aristotle said that one feature of adolescence is idealism. Thank goodness, they may make the world a better place than the one we are leaving to them.

One older daughter grasped this intuitively when she advised her father who was having a tough time managing two teenage sons, 'Dad, just get them doing things for others; they'll be fine.'

Turn good intentions into action

'Men were brought into existence for the sake of others, that they might do one another good.' CICERO, 106–43 BC

'Money is like muck … it is only of use if you spread it.' FRANCIS BACON, 1561–1626

'Only a life lived for others is a life worthwhile.' ALBERT EINSTEIN, 1879–1955

'In our era, the road to holiness necessarily passes through the world of action.' DAG HAMMARSKJOLD, 1905–1961, FIRST SECRETARY-GENERAL, UNITED NATIONS

12 Teach detachment from material things

'Beyond a certain minimum standard of living, all the studies show that happiness does not further increase as wealth increases.'

John Menadue, former Head of the Prime Minister's Department and CEO of Qantas

Graffiti along my favourite jogging route reads, 'I shop therefore I am'. Descartes would squirm! How enthusiastically did you take possession of your new car? What glossy magazines and mobiles catch your eye? Which advertisements? How therapeutic do you find shopping for clothes? Which websites do you visit? Do you buy or hope for expensive presents? Do you talk about food and wines with remarkable relish? How much do you worry about financial security? These factors will all influence whether your child will grow up in a materialistic environment. Try never to live the lie that the more you possess, the louder the music, or the more extreme the experience, the happier you become.

We adults can sometimes give all the wrong messages to our children. Marcus Aurelius, of *Gladiator* fame, reminds us that good times need not be expensive times: 'Remember this! Very little is needed to make a happy life.' The philosopher, Bertrand Russell, observed, 'It is preoccupation with possession, more than anything else, which prevents man from living freely and nobly.' Teach children to make use of whatever things they need, but not to put their hearts or their happiness in things. Teach *detachment*.

One man was reminiscing about his village in the Middle East: 'We used to be very happy. Though we were poor we would help each other. Now many receive money from rich relatives overseas and the homes are much better, but we don't help each other and we are not happy.' Students who have been on service projects in Sri Lankan fishing villages say the same thing, 'The people have practically nothing but they are so happy.'

Core values of children reflect core values of parents

- *'What do you want to be?' Year 4 boy: 'A millionaire!'*
- *To a son who is struggling in his Year 7 exams, Dad says, 'Don't worry. Exams don't last forever. You get a good job and then make lots of money.'*
- *Horrie in Year 3 was punched and given a bleeding nose by Alan in Year 6. In his defence, Alan said he wanted Horrie's mobile phone.*
- *'I've had the perfect birthday', a boy in Year 6 says, 'I got a trail bike and walkie talkies from New York.'*
- *Nick boasts he has been promised a red Ferrari if he is 'successful' in his end of school exams.*

A lesson from a child

'At a time when I was buying everything that opens and shuts for my son, I bought a very expensive train for him for his birthday. When I came back twenty minutes later, my son was having more fun playing with the box than the train that came in it.'

HENRI, FATHER OF THREE

Hook, Line and Lamborghini

Thierry tells students he meets on the train that his family does not have a car. They cannot believe it possible. The next day he confesses that he was fibbing. 'In fact', he says, 'my father has three Lamborghinis and a black Porsche'. The others drool over his good fortune. They readily believe that a family can own four luxury cars, but cannot conceive of a home without something out the front!

Detachment in one easy step

Vance, on the way from picking up his brand new sporty red Renault, called in at school to see a teacher. During the hour in which he was in discussion, someone ripped the lock out of the car door and tore the hi-fi from its dashboard niche. Vance's perplexed response on inspecting the damage: 'Well, it's a good way to learn detachment!'

13 Focus on causes and consequences

'Make it your business to know yourself. This is the most difficult lesson in the world.'

CERVANTES, 1547–1616

Lessons from the Temple

Teach children to know themselves, to reflect on the causes of their actions and on the effects they have on others. Whatever one's faith, the wisdom of the Lost in the Temple story repays a close reading. Do you know the scene? Mary and Joseph find Jesus deep in discussion with teachers in the Temple and she asks, 'Why have you done this? See how worried your father and I have been, looking for you.' The mother asks her twelve-year-old son to consider the causes and consequences of what he has done. In particular, Jesus's mother wants him to reflect on his motivations and on the impact of his actions on those who love him most. This is as close as Christians get to an example of perfect parenting.

Try to help your child think and reflect. It is much more important to get your twelve- or fourteen-year-old to accept ownership of his actions and their impact on others, rather than for you to be certain he is doing what he is told. A parent who insists on external conformity and who doesn't aim to build inner conviction is heading for possible tragedy. The two most important words on any practical parenting checklist are arguably *causes* and *consequences*. 'Force without reason falls of its own weight', wrote Horace, the canny old Roman soldier who fought with Brutus at Philippi and rose to be the great lyric poet of his times.

These are the types of questions to ask of a young person:

1 **Causes** Why have you done this? Think about your motivations. Were you acting freely? What was influencing you? Was it a decision or an impulse? Could you have exercised more personal responsibility?

2 **Consequences** What effects has your action had on the people around you? Do you understand the repercussions of this action? Do you understand the effect of your example? Think it through, for respect for others must underpin all we do. Never be afraid to look squarely at your actions, and if need be, undo them or make a good resolution for next time and carry it through.

Be professional

Professional skills transfer to parenting. If businesses need regular goal setting and evaluation of those goals, in the much more important task of parenting surely we should be reminding ourselves of our goals and action plans even more frequently. Be goal oriented. Set targets that can be evaluated. Maintain unity in the management team. Communicate with the stakeholders. Follow a consultative model. Lead by example. Be proactive. Is it right to be *less* professional in raising a family than we are in the workplace?

The challenge of owning one's actions

An eight-year-old girl who was discovered jumping up and down on the dining room table wails, 'It was an accident! It was an accident!'

***

'I went out to get something that had fallen out the window,' a twelve-year-old explains when pulled up for being outside the room. The reality was somewhat more complex. Yes, he had climbed out the window, but he had taken someone's things and put them on the window ledge, and then orchestrated a deliberate gag near the window with another boy, leading to the item being pushed out the window. Behind the action was a history of bullying and fun at others' expense.

***

'I got a detention because I blew my nose,' a thirteen-year-old student says glumly. The facts were a little different. A handkerchief was involved, but the punishment was for raucous well-constructed interruptions in class.

A CHECKLIST FOR CONSOLIDATING GOOD HABITS

We emphasise routines and consistency in the home.
We delegate even if it takes more time to get the job done.
We insist that our child acts with a loving intention.
We address bad behaviours before they become habits.
We find ways to help our child think for himself or herself … asking preferences, opinions and goals.
We each strive to give the best example we can, all the time.
We clearly teach what is right and wrong.
We focus on building up habits in our child's younger years.
We make character building the aim of our child's sport.
We turn parenting crises into opportunities to build character.
We greatly value sincerity in our home.
We correct small and large insincerity.
We are conscious of our own example in matters relating to sincerity and honesty.
We value greatly generosity in our family.
We teach a deep respect for others.
We have created a culture of generosity in the home.
We teach detachment from material things.
We strive for practical solidarity with those who are less fortunate.

Forging good habits

POINTS FOR REFLECTION

- Know your children's strengths and weaknesses.
- Realise that loving care for others underpins all virtue. The example of the affectionate love of parents for each other is important.
- Address issues – 'A consequence is worth a thousand words'.
- It's never too early to give a child good reasons.
- People *forget* what we say, they *remember* what they see, but they *learn* from what they do.

Level of development in your family					Priority areas
Well-developed	***Fair to middling***	***Fair***	***Much work needed***	***Non-existent***	

- Take up amateur psychology – address the needs of a child's mind and heart.
- Don't despise the small details.
- Keep a focus on sincerity and generosity.
- Don't allow your children to become well-programmed consumers. Advertisers and the media can be 'rivals for your children's hearts and minds' (Jim Stenson).

Learning from the Classics
Mum, can I go and hang out at the forum with the guys?
Not until you've helped your father fend off the barbarians.
Wilcox

PART 4
Raising teenagers with strength of character

Start early

Address the needs of teenage children

Reject any negative view of adolescence

Recognise potential

How to raise teenagers with strength of character

1. Own up to your innermost values
2. Show that your values bring you happiness
3. Realise that teenagers are changing on the inside first
4. Require teenagers to think, not to do
5. Help your teenager internalise the process of developing good habits
6. Find new ways to keep communicating
7. Address issues
8. Explain reasons
9. Don't underestimate the impact of the peer group
10. Look for reinforcement from your son's or daughter's school
11. Seek out mentors who have the confidence of your teenager
12. Focus on resilience
13. Prepare your son or daughter for relationships and sexuality
14. Give your teenager affection, affection, and more affection
15. Teach peace in the face of the very greatest challenges

'Always be a man, not a boy gone astray.'

ROBBIE ROBERTSON, *ENDLESS HIGHWAY*

Remember the bumper sticker, 'Live long enough to take revenge on your teenagers'? In our culture we fear adolescence. Statistics for accidents in the first years of driving, precocious sexual activity, and for self-harm, are certainly a serious concern. We parrot terms like 'teenage rebellion', 'disconnectedness' or 'generation gap'. And because of all this negative press, we can miss the most beautiful dimensions of adolescence.

In 1993 I was most fortunate to attend a course in San Francisco entitled 'Parents and their Adolescent Children', where I heard David Isaacs arguing that adolescence is a time of the most far-reaching personal exploration, and that this reality is by far the most important feature of these years, eclipsing all the superficial features of adolescence. He spoke of the growing awareness in teenage years of autonomy and personal values. He insisted that adolescence is the time when a young person settles on the values that will take him or her through life, and he even suggested that until young people develop these convictions, they effectively don't leave adolescence. Perhaps Germaine Greer was walking a parallel thought line when she quipped, 'Girls grow up to be young women; boys grow up to be 6' 3". There are certainly some big kids around us, with egos unreconciled to a body that is not what it used to be, and fifty-somethings who dress and act more like teenagers, and married men and women unable to deliver total commitment to their partner.

Central to David Isaacs's advice to parents is that they must not do the thinking for their teenage children. 'Require teenagers to think, not to do', he insists. Give them lots of decision-making practice. Encourage them to match their actions to their values, a prerequisite for peace of soul and happiness in life.

The two discoveries of adolescence

1. The *discovery of self*, the personal world that is proper to human existence. 'I am a person, with my own mind, my own heart, my own personality.'
2. The *discovery of the values* that the young person chooses to underpin his or her life and of personal freedom and responsibility. 'I am free to take my life in the direction I want, and I decide to base my life on certain principles.'

Your goal as a parent is to hand over the wheel safely to a well-prepared, self-disciplined driver. Never has there been a truer description of adolescence than that written by the great Plutarch: 'For intelligent people the passage from childhood to adulthood is not an abandonment of rules, but a change of ruler'. The great challenge in raising teenagers is to bring them to responsible autonomy – to teach them self-management. Otherwise, long-term happiness will be very elusive.

How sad it is when children come off the rails. After an apparently model childhood they seriously rebel, start to deceive, and seem to fall so far short of what they can be. In their early years perhaps they were *well trained* how to behave, but the motivation was coming from outside themselves – their actions were not springing from within – and as a consequence their good behaviours were easily abandoned, perhaps because the poor example of others flew in under the parental radar. In life, those who are not masters of themselves, those who are not *self-possessed*, fall under the sway of others.

Perpetual adolescence

David Isaacs talks of 45-year-olds who are still essentially teenagers, because they *behave* like teenagers. Most of us have more or less opted for a particular set of values by the time we are coming to the end of our teens. But there are some who for decades toss restlessly between self-centredness and the dedication to others that underpins loving relationships and, ultimately, happiness.

Start early

'Treat a man as he is and he will remain as he is; treat him as he can and should be and he will become what he can and should be.'

GOETHE, 1749–1832

Effective parenting of teenagers begins in the cradle, if not earlier. Don't start when your son or daughter is twelve. Most of the hard yards are done before teenage hormones kick in.

Upbringing is not about cloning children to conform with your wishes. You are raising them to run their own lives so the less you run their lives, even when they are small, the better. Don't over-manage even young children. From the time your child is very young, visualise the young man or woman you are seeking to raise, and foster those strengths of character, consistently and resolutely:

1. **Don't be negative.** Start with what you admire in your son's or daughter's character. From the early years, make praise very specific and criticism positive and constructive. Without habits of parent–child affection and focused attention in the pre-teen years, the parent–teen bonds will strain or snap.
2. **Carry with you habitually a deep peace and calm.** Lead by example. Show that commitments to others bring great serenity; as the engraving on an old sundial says, '*horas non numero nisi serenas*' (loosely translated, 'I am only interested in calm and serene hours'). What a great shame when young children fail to learn that it is generosity that brings happiness; it is so much harder to pick this up later.
3. **Don't do the thinking for them.** If they don't have practice thinking for themselves as younger children, they won't be able to do it as teenagers, and you won't think of giving it priority when they are teenagers.

4 **Give reasons, starting from when your child is very young.** Young people need a comprehensive *reference manual* if they are to run their own lives. Consult the preferences and opinions even of younger children whenever possible, and explain simply and honestly the *why* of decisions you have made in their interests – generally because there has been physical or moral danger involved in following the child's preferred direction.

5 **Expect responsibility.** Don't let your son or daughter out of consequences they have brought on themselves. They have to pay their debts, make the apology or submit the assignment. Don't fight their battles for them. In teenage years, life will bring challenges for which they have to be ready. The principle also applies to work: if you fail to teach a young child the importance of responsibility in finishing jobs, don't expect assignments to take priority in teenage years.

6 **Foster a healthy hardiness so that your child learns a degree of self-control.** There are alcoholics who grew up in teetotalling households and alcoholics whose parents gave them moderate amounts of alcohol. The key issue is whether a young person has learnt habits of self-control.

7 **Talk honestly to younger children about relationships and sexuality.** You have a real and pressing duty to ready your child for the complex but positive challenges of sexual attraction. How many marriages would be saved if children were better attuned to the duties that relationships bring.

In summary, a golden rule of raising teenagers is to get in early!

Don't baby your teenager

'The sooner you treat your son as a man, the sooner he will be one.'

JOHN DRYDEN, 1631–1700

Address the needs of teenage children

'Do not permit what you disapprove of ... Be conscious that "no" is also a loving word, and a necessary means for children's growth in self-control.'

JAMES STENSON, SCHOOL PRINCIPAL AND AUTHOR

It can help to look on your parenting as the task of addressing the needs of children, their current needs and their longer-term needs:

1 **Provide for the safety of your teenage children.** Clear limits are essential. Say no to activities that have the potential for physical or moral danger and to situations in which they may be dangerously out of their depth. Be critical of your own decision-making ... yes may be an easier answer but you have a solemn duty to guide this young person who lacks the life experience to recognise the bear pit in the path ahead and the bear that is hiding behind the tree. It makes no sense to allow sixteen-year-olds unrestricted and unsupervised social experiences. It makes no sense to allow your daughter to be travelling in cars at night with a person you hardly know.

Technology and teenagers

Technology brings terrific advantages and significant risks. Maximise the advantages and set parameters to avoid unnecessary risks. *Agree ahead of time* on reasonable guidelines for mobile phones, computer use, family mealtimes free of distraction, etc.

2 **Provide for your teenager's emotional needs.** Adolescence brings emotional turmoil at times. We have all been there. The changes of adolescence can trigger a lack of confidence that is played out in various ways:

- introversion
- moodiness

- compensatory behaviours to address a young person's negative self-perception, e.g. changes in eating habits, acting out to draw attention
- depression, based on a perceived powerlessness to change one's lot
- feelings of being misunderstood or rejected at home or at school.
- It is the *duty* of a parent to give emotional support to a child, not the other way around. Are you affectionate with your teenager even when your child does something you disapprove of or doesn't seem to reciprocate your efforts? No cold shoulders or resentment! Above all, model the *emotional stability* your son or daughter themselves need. Like a reforming alcoholic, 'Fake it till you make it'.
- Lead the way in your own relationship. Your child must have the utter confidence that love never runs out, that it is *for keeps*. By the unconditional love parents have for each other, they show their child that he or she will always be loved no matter what.

3 **Address essential long-term needs.** Foster a young person's capacity to *act* effectively in their lives. As discussed in Part 2, nurture *strong habits* of:

- sound judgement, including critical thinking and effective decision-making
- self-control, responsibility and fortitude – the other three cardinal virtues that help us act decisively and take the knocks of life
- love for others – an utter determination to do good to others in life
- deep humility because we are creatures who have duties and commitments to others, to our creator and

to all mankind – spiritual values bolster resilience and add an extra layer of charity to the motivation underpinning what we do.

Bottom lines in parenting teenagers

Help your teenager to:

- **Get the *head* right** – to learn right and wrong, build sound *values* and convictions, and a love for truth … ultimately to learn to *think for themselves*. This is where sincerity comes in.
- **Get the *heart* right** – to learn to *love*, to build strong personal relationships at human and spiritual levels, and to give of themselves in those relationships. Here is the place for generosity.
- **Get it right in habitual actions** – to build up the full range of *virtues*, personal qualities and habitual ways of behaving; to learn to be self-directing, and to make mature use of their freedom.

Teenage brain: a work in progress

Neurophysiologists now know that sectors of the brain undergo substantial development specifically during adolescence, facilitating new skills and greater self-control provided that we capitalise on these pathways to build explicit strategies of self-management. Dr Judith Rapoport and her colleagues were surprised to discover bursts of grey matter building in the first MRI longitudinal study of teenagers' developing brains. The development centred in the frontal lobe areas dedicated to planning, impulse control and reasoning. When your teenager acts very impulsively, teach him or her strategies to think before acting, and have confidence that the brain is also doing its bit.

Think about it!

'The best bred horses are spirited and impetuous. If they are broken in when they are young, they become more manageable, and better than any others; but if they grow up unbroken, they are very difficult to control and worse than any others.'

Xenophon

Reject any negative view of adolescence

'You think this is bad, wait until the next four are all teenagers.'

FOURTEEN-YEAR-OLD FRAN, THE ELDEST OF SEVEN,
AFTER AN ARGUMENT WITH HER PARENTS

Adolescent years are a marvellous time! Look beyond the superficial features of the age, the self-absorption and moodiness, the insecurity and impressionability, the wanting to be noticed, the emotional rollercoaster. Don't overreact to the rebelliousness, the lack of motivation and laziness, the need for affection and attention.

These surface features of adolescence have *always* been apparent. In the *Odyssey*, Homer wrote that a young person will try to 'break the rules', that he has 'a mind that is quicker, but his judgement is not so sound'. Elsewhere he wrote simply, 'young people are thoughtless as a rule'. Aristotle described youth as permanently 'in a state resembling intoxication', and he noted that 'young men have strong passions and tend to gratify them indiscriminately'.

Sound too familiar?

'I see no hope for the future of our people if they are dependent on the frivolous youth of today, for certainly all youth are reckless beyond words ... when I was young we were taught to be discreet and respectful of elders, but the present youth are exceeding wise and impatient of restraints.'

HESIOD, C. 700 BC

'The children now love luxury; they show disrespect for elders and love chatter in place of exercise. Children are tyrants, not the servants of their households. They no longer rise when their elders enter the room. They contradict their parents, chatter before company, gobble up dainties at the table, cross their legs and tyrannise their teachers.'

SOCRATES, 469–399 BC

Teenagers: 'prodigal in pleasures, skittish, and in need of a bridle.'

PLUTARCH, 46–120

The Romans knew that, like their home town, character is not built in a day. Reflecting on youth, the ex-slave, Publilius Syrus, said, 'There is no fruit that is not bitter before it is ripe.' Here was a Roman who knew that, like his home town, character is not built in a day. Pliny described the life of a young person as 'somewhat turbulent and disorganised' whereas Cicero preferred to focus on the refrigerator. He joked that he was 'terrified' of his nephew's appetite. Young people have always been like this.

Superficial features of adolescence

- rebelliousness
- self-absorption
- introspection
- laziness
- lack of motivation
- yearning for affection
- impressionability
- wanting to be noticed
- lack of perspective
- poor emotional control
- moodiness
- insecurity
- overconfidence.

Relax: adolescent rebellion is essentially positive

Even when the Battle for Baghdad starts over having to do the dishes, we must not forget that adolescent rebellion is pre-eminently positive. At its heart it is the natural process by which we all learn to stand alone, to think for ourselves.

As adults we regard all forms of patronising and over-management as inappropriate. Yet adolescents are adults in the making and it is good and natural that they should want more and more freedom; it is a prerequisite for a mature personality.

Parents should not be scared when they observe a growing independent spirit in their son or daughter. They should not react with panic and legislate rules as if their teenager was still a child. All forms of over-management or coercion are an infringement of legitimate autonomy. It is counterproductive to compel older children to do anything.

Recognise potential

'Keep away from people who try to belittle your ambitions. Small people always do that, but the really great make you feel that you, too, can become great.'

MARK TWAIN, 1835–1910

Why do we so undersell teenagers? How little we sometimes expect. Consider this: several eighteen-year-old young women carry out deliberate, ongoing, after-dark, anonymous harassment of a student they don't like and a teacher. They are found out. One parent, indignant at the school's suggestion that such behaviour could merit expulsion, lobbies board members. The other parents refuse to be drawn into the issue, figuring that if an adult could lose a job for such behaviour, then eighteen-year-old students are well old enough to be accountable.

How is it that we let children develop personality sapping behaviours right before our eyes? In some homes, when guests come for dinner, the teenager in the family eats customarily in front of the television. In others, parents learn to accommodate cynical back chat; or successive bad reports from school merely attract the predictable parental clichés, which have absolutely no effect. Nor is it good training for future family commitments for your teenage boy to sit in the back seat immersed in headphones while you dutifully chauffeur him.

We all know how impressionable we were as teenagers, and how we could follow infatuations and fads, yet some fads are more dangerous than others, some ways of dressing are more provocative than others, some behaviours are more antisocial than others. Parents have a duty to educate children in these situations. If we do not fight the little habits that are being formed, they will set rock hard and become impossible to shift without a gigantic act of the will … and whose fault will that be?

The words of legendary Rugby League coach, Jack Gibson, 'I don't want any of you people looking back and wondering how good you could have been', are eminently applicable in the home. Parents have a sacred duty to do their very best to ensure that the young persons in their care bring to reality the marvellous potential that lies in each – potential for love, generous relationships and happiness. Each child, in his or her own way, is called to greatness. But whether they ever get there is all too dependent on the head start they receive.

Never underestimate the raw material in a young person

- At twelve Augustus gave the oration at his father's funeral and Jesus coped alone in a city for three days with no problem.
- Genghis Khan commanded the union of his clans when he was thirteen.
- In many cultures it has been common for girls to marry by thirteen or fourteen.
- Pompey waged a successful civil war at seventeen.
- At the end of his adolescent years, Michelangelo sculpted the Pieta.

Trust your teenager

My Adam was in Year 9. We were becoming a little concerned about his lack of motivation (particularly concerning school studies) and were absolutely despairing of how he would be able to organise himself in his future working life. It was a typically busy morning rush, with four children at four schools and thus four school buses to meet! Adam was interested in playing roller hockey with a friend after school and was not keen on having to go on the bus with his hockey stick.

I grumbled a little and said okay. Later I noticed he was going around the living room opening curtains and doing the usual tidying jobs that I do before leaving in the morning. As I washed up I noticed him take his bag, skates and stick out to the car so that he was ready to go!

Hmmmmm, I thought, why do I worry?

Katrina, mother of two sons and two daughters

How to raise teenagers with strength of character

The following points apply principles of character education to raising teenagers. The focus is very much on fostering in these adults-in-the-making the *sound judgement* they will need for *self-directed actions.*

1 Own up to your innermost values

'Who has deceived thee so often as thyself?'

Benjamin Franklin, 1706–1790

Adolescents are sizing up their parents' values. Without thinking too much about the theory, teenagers are deciding what attitudes in life will bring happiness. All parents need to be deeply honest with themselves so that the values they wish to pass on are in fact the values they live by. Children see through lip-service to values.

> **Know thyself**
>
> *'The easiest thing of all is to deceive oneself, for what a man wishes he generally believes to be true.'*
>
> Demosthenes, 384–322 BC
>
> *'I have been a selfish being all my life, in practice though not in principle.'*
>
> Mr D'Arcy, in Jane Austin's *Pride and Prejudice*
>
> *'Look on your family budget as a numerical measure of your family's values.'*
>
> Professor David Isaacs

David Isaacs illustrates this principle with a story about a father very disillusioned by the behaviour of his son. The father is a high-powered executive making a trillion so that he can get away on weekends to his speedboat and weekender. The son makes no effort at school and skives off to the surf as often as he can get a classmate to cover for him. Although their behaviour seems very different, they are motivated by identical values: each wants life to be as pleasurable as possible. The means they use to achieve their goals differ, but the goals are the same. The conclusion is bone-jarring for some parents.

We adults must look at ourselves critically. What is the real message we give when we overeat, when we lose our tempers, when we talk badly of others, when we arrive late night after night for the family meal? What are the real values we are communicating? And consider the spiritual fallout also: any parent who professes faith in God but is constantly stressed lives out an evident lack of confidence in God's daily providence. Children may hear the talk, but they will walk the path of underlying convictions. If we want to succeed in passing on the deepest, most cherished beliefs of our lives, we must ensure that those convictions are not smothered under the day-to-day pressures of work and survival.

Try not to make an exception of yourself; you must demand of yourself in the same areas you demand of your children. Television viewing habits can only be changed at some personal cost. Even our habits of parenting – our overreactions, mistrust, inept ways of making conversation with a ten-year-old, confrontational response to school reports – these habits must be changed at considerable personal effort. And the older we are, the harder it is to change habits.

The chocolate and the ice cream

Compare the reactions of Family A and Family B.

In Family A, with dad's knowledge, a large block of chocolate is eaten by the kids on the afternoon of purchase. There are serious recriminations. No more chocolate is to be bought this month. Dad is castigated by a cranky mum in front of the family.

Father of Family B discovers that all the ice cream has been given to the kids that afternoon by their mother and now there is none for dessert despite the fact that there is a visitor. There is a general laugh about how delicious the ice cream was. Alternate dessert plans are quickly put in place.

Let's be honest

'Out of all the things that you have to do in the afternoon, what do you think is the most important?'

'Helping mum, but dad thinks football training is!' Peter, in Year 4, replies.

Learning from anorexia

The previous eighteen months had been a living nightmare. Our fourteen-year-old daughter's weight had fallen to 34 kilograms and she was in hospital to keep her alive. Carly fitted all the criteria for anorexia nervosa: *teenager, female, intellectually gifted, an overwhelming perfectionist. What mistakes had we made to cause this thing? Tess, our elder daughter, Beth and myself were all well and truly in bondage to its psychological effects as well! The crisis had consumed the whole family. Our incessant prayer seemed to no avail. Things just got worse.*

What set Carly free from the bondage of anorexia was not medical care, although it did sustain her life for a time. Her cure and complete restoration was a direct result of reaching a heartfelt realisation that God loved her unconditionally; that she would no longer have to strive to achieve in order to gain acceptance from others. She understood that her God-given, legitimate needs for acceptance, significance and security could only be fulfilled in an intimate relationship with Him.

Through Carly's anorexia, Beth and I learnt many things about parenting, but there is one crucial lesson that towers above all others. Children are entrusted to us for a time, and our task is to guide them to become what Father-God wants them to become, and not what we demand that they become. Then and only then will they be able to produce the spiritual fruit with eternal consequences both for them and those they will touch in their own lives. Demanding of our children that they reach their 'full potential' in purely human terms is to give them a burden that is ***of this world****. This is what we have learnt from this crisis.*

Carly recently completed a degree in Media and Communications and is now presenting the news for a major radio network.

Doug and Beth, parents of two beautiful daughters

2 Show that your values bring you happiness

'Why should children be happy with their lot when parents complain about theirs?'

Barbara Holborow, former Children's Court Magistrate

Your way of life must bring you happiness … attractive, big-hearted happiness. If not, your child may well say: 'Mum and Dad, I love you, but I can't live by your values. I need something that's going to make me happy in life.' In homes where a parent is chronically dissatisfied, cranky or critical, why should any child want to imitate that parent?

Example alone is not enough. We have all met hard-working parents who seem to have lazy sons. Every church has parents whose children wouldn't think of coming with the family on Sundays. I have met health-conscious parents whose daughters smoke, drink and take drugs. How can this be?

No, it's not easy

I know of a couple who were determined not to let television into the home. It was a Pyrrhic victory. After the wall finally came down, the family lounge room featured no fewer than two broken televisions and another that was being worked to death. One daughter, after she moved out, invested several pay packets on a wide screen Rolls Royce of televisions. Another child would often be watching the TV for hours in the middle of the day.

***

A more serious tale. Another family brought up their daughter in a strict religious community that required the family and children to dedicate the bulk of each Sunday to family activities and family worship. The daughter in the family grew up, married young, slipped into depression, cheated on her husband within two years and left him.

Talk and example are not enough. It would be absurd for a father to nag about the need for hard work, and then for his children to see him chronically worrying about financial security, and taking pills for his ulcer. Hard work must be seen to bring happiness, not anxiety – not the satisfaction of affluence, but the happiness of inner contentment. Very different.

And children have to sense that dad is somehow happier when he is *not* dependent on a hamburger or a thick shake. They have to see that mum isn't cranky at rush hour each night, but cheerful and positive about life. They have to see that dad comes in from work with a smile on his face. Day after day, year after year, this is obviously a big ask.

In cheerful homes the present and the future are important, not the past. Look forward, not back. Children need to see us looking on the positive and cheerful side of life and that the values we are teaching do work for ourselves first of all. Otherwise why should they pay the least attention?

Possessions and happiness

'A magnificent house, massive wealth, a splendid genealogy, and high office, eloquence and fluency, are all incapable of giving life the degree of fair and calm weather that is afforded by a mind which is untainted by bad actions and intentions and which bases life on a character that is calm and clear.'

PLUTARCH, 46–120

*'At school we tell children to be the **best** in maths and the **best** in football. In adult life we aim to have the **best** house, the **best** car. Where does **happiness** come into this? Why don't we aim for happiness?'*

ROY, PARAMEDIC AND GROUNDSMAN, AND FATHER OF FOUR

'I like Mr Q. My last teacher never smiled.'

SCOTT, EIGHT YEARS OLD

'I'm never going to have a family, because all we do at home is fight.'

BRIDIE, SIXTEEN YEARS OLD, TO HER MOTHER

3 Realise that teenagers are changing on the inside first

'Peace cannot be kept by force. It can only be achieved by understanding.'

ALBERT EINSTEIN, 1879–1955

Many parents seem to underestimate their teenager's *developmental* age by a year or more. They forcefully correct their teenage son or daughter in front of younger siblings, and even friends. Conversations boil over in the blink of an eye with parents seemingly on a different frequency. Family plans for the weekend made without any attempt at consultation cause further friction. The 'external rulers', as Plutarch called parents, call the shots in a most patronising way. And meanwhile, the 'internal ruler', the teenager, impatient for independence, is pushing the envelope continuously.

Just because your thirteen-year-old is not speaking about her anxiety doesn't mean that it is not a *big* issue in her mind. Fathers, particularly, can be almost totally insensitive to the fact that this twelve-year-old girl is now a very different person to the pretty little girl in the party dress only two years ago. That fourteen-year-old boy now has plenty on his mind and nobody else is privy to it. But three years ago all he seemed to think about was footy on Saturdays and Harry Potter the rest of the week.

It is in the early teenage years that our inner life develops. Think back. When we were thirteen or fourteen, we had our moody and self-absorbed moments and at the same time we were forming opinions on everything. Human nature doesn't change. Insensitive parents assume that their thirteen-year-old is just a hungrier version of the little boy who believed in Santa Claus and tooth fairies. If they don't start understanding their teenager, they will grow further and further distant. Parents can fail to grasp how quickly the changes come once kids get over the twelve-year dotted line. It is in the mind of the young person that the biggest changes take place. Just because your introspective daughter is not saying much, it doesn't mean she is not reflecting on things a great deal.

Lessons from Warhammer

I know one fourteen-year-old whose hobby is painting Warhammer figures. His intricate collection is his pride. It has steadily grown since he started collecting them when he was ten and he still spends hours in his room painting them. In fact most of his behaviours are the same as when he was in Year 5. He still plays soccer. He is generally polite and hard working. He is a good listener, but minds his own counsel.

Just because this teenager seems to behave the same as he did when he was younger, don't miss the great changes that are taking place on the inside. Don't underestimate the maturity and the capacity for independent thought and action this young man now possesses. Otherwise, the war will definitely come, and it won't be with painted soldiers.

When teenagers complain that their parents don't understand them, they can be completely correct. Parents can fall into the obvious trap of thinking that the main changes in adolescence are merely physical. But by the time the physical changes are becoming obvious, other profound changes on the inside have already been setting in stone.

Don't get distracted

Some parents get distracted by long hours at work, by their own relationship problems, by financial pressures, and the myriad other adult concerns.

A month is a long time in a teenager's mind. By the time parents refocus on family, that little girl in the party dress is not acting anything like a young lady at parties – but they don't know about that. And that boy with the yo-yo is now reading magazines that degrade women instead of doing his homework – but they don't know much about that either. Does your teenager let you into his or her world? Remember, you cannot force the door.

4 Require teenagers to think, not to do

'A gentleman, well studied in literature, and abiding by the normal expectations of good behaviour, will not go very wrong.'

CONFUCIUS, 551–479 BC

Give your reasons, and then give them space. Don't oblige conformity, but do expect soon-to-be-adults to reflect on their consistency with the values they profess. Often, they will realise that the media hype or popularity sham they have been following are just counterfeits of real values. *With our love* we must encourage children to recognise the half-truths around them in the entertainment and consumer worlds.

> *'You must cudgel your brains for some way of destroying this mob in your house. You are no longer a child. Put childish thoughts away.'*
>
> THE GODDESS URGES ODYSSEUS'S SON, IN HOMER'S *ODYSSEY*, C. 700 BC

Don't table-thump your child into submission. Your efforts will be self-defeating. Coercion is contrary to nature: 'A young man must be overcome by reason, not by force', a Roman schoolteacher once wrote. You either help teenagers think for themselves or you are out of the game. Many parent–child relationships take their pear shape far into adult years.

How many children conform while they live at home and then cut loose? How many teenagers do the right thing only when they are being watched? Why do so many end up in thought-dulling substance abuse or in short-term relationships that bring long-term scars?

Blind Freddy could tell us that when young people *without* convictions are exposed to moral dangers through a questionable peer group they *will not* have the strength or experience to make the right choices. When moral or physical safety is in the balance, making mistakes is *not* a good way to learn. There has to be a better way. Sound moral preparation, not moral risk-taking, is the answer.

Explain reasons, but don't get locked into an argument. Teach critical thinking. Unless there is clear and present, physical or moral, danger, or unless you have good reasons to *think* there is danger, reasons which you explain, let Tim or Sally-Anne decide for themselves to get that job after school or buy that old VW. Give them information to help them make up their own minds and then help them take on board the *consequences* of their choices. 'Tim, if you work in that pet shop you will need to get yourself there and back. Sally-Anne, if you want that bomb it will cost every cent you have earned in three years at the café. You will then work all weekend to pay for petrol, and it is unlikely to pass rego in four months time, but the choice is yours'; or 'Sal, I would love to help you get that car, but before I can say yes we will need to clock up at least 50 more hours of driving lessons. Inexperience is always dangerous on the roads. When do we start?'

Experiences are much more powerful than passive lessons

'Tell me, I forget.
Show me, I remember.
Involve me, I understand.'

Confucius, 551–479 BC

***

One young teacher following his last year at school spent two of his summer months in India on a parish promoted trip. Those days with Mother Teresa changed his life.

***

One father, a land valuer, decided to have his teenage boys accompany him on a professional walk along a notorious street early one Sunday morning. They saw the young people in the doorways and the broken glass. They smelt the vomit and the stale beer. Then, over a milkshake, they talked about what they had witnessed.

'Divide each difficulty into as many parts as is feasible and necessary to resolve it.'

Rene Descartes, 1596–1650

Elementary School No. 126

Effective education needs to be genuinely personal. During a mid-year break I attended a conference of schools in the United States. When my bus passed Elementary School No. 126 on the way in from New York airport, I knew I was not exactly in the land of personalised education!

Let us reject the ridiculous assumption that children get schooled automatically once they are sitting in classrooms, or that schools educate children in spite of what happens at home. Every young person deserves our dedicated personal attention.

Personal attention starts first of all in the family and is founded on the loving affection between children and parents; and this personal interest must extend to school and work environments. Without such attention, many children will fall far short of potential, and some will be irreparably damaged.

Leaving school?

The law requires nobody to stay at school after turning 15 years more or less. A student who decides to continue at school *must* knuckle down. How counterproductive for a young person to spend several more years at school entrenching habits of laziness and irresponsibility that will continue to dog them well into adulthood.

Don't make excuses for a child capable of achieving acceptable application grades in every subject. It is not your problem. Communicate the urgency. Help your son or daughter think things through, to set realistic goals for themselves and throw themselves into their studies – or find something else they want to throw their energies into.

Life will present greater problems than this.

Some mums cannot do enough ...

'Thou shalt never forget what thy mother has done for thee ... when thou didst enter the school and was instructed in the writings, she came daily with bread and beer from her house.'

Eny, Egyptian scribe

5 Help your teenager internalise the process of developing good habits

'It is no profit to have learnt well, if we neglect to do well.'

PUBLILIUS SYRUS, 1ST CENTURY BC

A young man undergoing counselling for sexual abuse was described by his psychologist as being quite cerebral in the way he dealt with the issues, unable to empathise with those he had abused. Morals in our heads but *not in our hearts* are pretty well useless. It is no advantage knowing all the answers if we do not live them. Some of the greatest criminals knew just how wrong their actions were. Macbeth saw the evil of his actions but he still wanted to kill the king. The essential challenge in teenage years is *internalising* the values that have been learnt. Good values must lead to a good heart, and to habitually good choices.

There are two main mechanisms for turning values into good habitual behaviour:

1 We lead younger children to have good habits through consistent routines, clear expectations, and good examples in everything and from everyone. If the family provides a truly loving example, and if the competing influences are kept in harness, children learn almost by osmosis to imbue their own actions, in turn, with love.

2 When we miss out on this first round, when we already can see the bad habits we are developing, we still get another chance, thank goodness. By reflecting on values, by setting our own goals, and then by plugging away until we consolidate the new behaviours, we get there. This process is one of internalising convictions and arduously correcting personal behaviours.

Therefore, with teenagers in the house, maintain the orderly routines and clear expectations, but give much more attention to nurturing motives. Leave your son or daughter free, and encourage them to measure their own actions against the clear standards of right and wrong you have taught them from childhood. Don't make decisions for them. Give them practice in making up their own minds and then debrief them with abundant affection when they make mistakes. Provide loving encouragement and confidence they will get there. Help them to see, as Aristotle simply put it, 'Happiness depends on ourselves'.

Stopping to reflect – a mark of maturity

An ex-student, Takuya, sent this email: 'I am turning twenty on August 12 and I believe it is one of my turning points in my life. I want to end my teenage years with a trip alone looking back at my past and thinking about my coming future.'

From the conviction that young people must do their own thinking he was off to take stock of his life.

Some two thousand three hundred years ago Socrates told the story of Heracles who, like Takuya, '... was setting out from childhood to manhood, at the age when the young become independent and show whether they are going to approach life by the path of goodness or by the path of wickedness. He went out to a quiet spot and sat down considering which way he should take.'

Echoes of Robert Frost in the woods! Every young person could do worse than to retreat from the noise of daily life to reflect on what he or she really is looking for.

'Whom do I call educated? First, those who manage well the circumstances they encounter day by day. Next, those who are decent and honourable in their intercourse with all men, bearing easily and good naturedly what is offensive in others and being as agreeable and reasonable to their associates as is humanly possible to be ... those who hold their pleasures always under control and are not ultimately overcome by misfortunes ... those who are not spoiled by their successes, who do not desert their true selves but hold ground steadfastly as wise and sober-minded men.'

Socrates, 469–399 BC

6 Find new ways to keep communicating

'Most adolescent problems can be alleviated or rectified by correcting tensions in the parent-child relationship.'

DR ROSS CAMPBELL, *HOW TO REALLY LOVE YOUR TEENAGER*

Respect your child's right to self-determination. Don't just tell them what their goals should be. Don't try to manipulate your child into a career path, a subject choice or your favourite sport. No matter how much energy it takes, engage with that young person, establish mutual admiration and respect, and nurture the internalised attitudes they will need as adults.

Consensus on effective parent–child communication

1. **Talk less to be heard more.**
   'Attentive silence is the best way to evoke a child's feelings.' Avoid futile practices: the lecture, the cliché, the heated word.
2. **Give a fair hearing.**
   'Keep your mouth closed until the child closes his.'
3. **Practise your timing.**
   Know when the 'prime times of communication' are.
4. **Say it without words.**
   Give affection. 'Affection is continuous communication.' 'The "heart" of a parent is usually more important than child rearing "mechanics".'
5. **Seek your child's opinion.**
   'While in most cases parents retain the final say, kids better accept decisions that they were consulted about and see themselves as a valued part of family decisions.'

The engine room of raising teenagers is this *strong parent–child rapport* where issues can be discussed in intimacy, trust and depth. Foster behaviour that flows from the deepest respect for others. Without an affectionate connection you will be excluded from your teenager's heart and oblivious to their deepest hopes and worries. Never nag. Rely on heart-to-heart conversations that help you *understand* what your son or daughter is thinking.

If you are your son's and daughter's confidant, you can be the decisive influence in their lives

- Your relationship depends a great deal on your habits of relaxed talk in pre-teen years and on the connections you have established.
- Chat often – at least weekly one on one; the art is in the timing. Someone once said that women prefer to talk face to face, while men look in the same direction. See if it works. Be generous with your time; that is a prerequisite.
- Listen more than you talk. Remember, if you want them as adults to come asking your advice, they need to develop that habit now.
- Rely on occasional, deep heart-to-heart conversations that help you understand what your son or daughter is thinking; don't just tell them what to think. They must reflect on what is happening and set their own goals, not your goals.
- When you have to raise difficult issues, don't criticise from outside. Think the best of them. Don't judge intentions, talk about the facts.
- Talk about the big issues – life and death, love and relationships, freedom, spiritual values, and love for truth.
- Open up about your own life and childhood. Teach your son or daughter to recognise his or her strengths, and also shortcomings, by talking about your own battles and discoveries. Pass on the toughest life lessons you have learnt: set strong convictions and ideals rock hard in a street-wise shrewdness.

Open your heart on paper

Letters and emails can strike deeper chords. On 9/11 one young man who had been near the towers wrote to his father:

'The sights that I saw during the day were very disturbing … I appreciate all the emails and phone calls from everyone and it reminds me of how many good friends and loving family I have. I felt particularly mortal yesterday and was reminded of the priorities in life and how much you all mean to me.'

Raising touchy topics with teens

Raise the topic and weather the initial reaction. Don't react emotionally, but don't back off the need to air the issue. When they settle down, talk calmly.

7 Address issues

'Life is not a video, you can't replay it. You can't put it on pause. When it is gone, it is gone. We only get one shot.'

PHIL GOULD, NSW STATE OF ORIGIN COACH

Like loose bolts on jumbo jets, problems get bigger when we don't address them. Stay calm. Focus on the issue. Make a plan. Normally, nobody should be better placed to help a child through a crisis than that child's parent.

Inappropriate behaviours bring unpleasant consequences to the person who does them. Help your teenager see that it is not good for anyone to develop sloppy or selfish habits. It is not your problem; it is first of all his or her problem. This teenager will be the biggest loser if the behaviour does not change. A succession of poor school application grades will mean that your child is failing to grow in responsibility – an issue with very serious consequences for any young person down the track.

When we want to change an entrenched pattern of behaviour, the rule is to substitute a new zeal and enthusiasm in its place. It is not enough just to lecture fourteen-year-old John about how he must perform in all his assignments. He may say he will try, but entrenched bad habits are harder to shift than this. Close support is needed. He must be put into a situation where he is *enthusiastic* about the new task. And sometimes it is simply better to leave school and go on to really attractive activities.

When behaviours are deeply entrenched – drug-taking, sexual addiction, alarming peer influences, apathy with respect to the most obvious responsibilities, chronic insolence – extreme measures may be needed to rescue a young person. A temporary life change may be an essential aspect of a 'treatment' plan. Drug habits require disconnection from the peer group. Think about moving house to the country or have the family join you for a business exchange overseas. Your child's good heart and good intentions will overcome vices, but only if the old behaviours are suspended. *Buy time* to set up new patterns of repeated behaviours. Be very creative. Parents must not begrudge personal hardship when a child's welfare is at stake. Eventually a young person will find peace if he or she has learnt how to be sincere and learnt to keep getting up again, despite failures.

At *any* suggestion of clinical depression – changes in eating and sleeping patterns, children withdrawing from those closest to them, any substance abuse or other escapist behaviour, evidence of self-harm, vague references to dying – it is *essential* and *urgent* to seek professional help.

Parties

The following guidelines can save much angst. Talk about them before emotions are involved:

- In pre-teen years parents do well to avoid creating precedents of large parties, sleep-overs, excessive frequency of parties, parties in the weeks prior to exams, etc.
- Prefer a natural and inclusive family approach whenever possible – invite parents and their children.
- Habitually keep the scale small: numbers should be capped at around twenty. Small parties integrate adults and younger people far better, make supervision easier, and put less peer pressure on class members to go.
- Have a guest list and invitations on paper.
- Have a 'house supplies' policy for alcohol, with everyone asked to remain after they arrive.
- Ensure pick-ups are at an hour that respects the rights of all.
- Have other parents over to help.
- When possible, keep parties to holidays.

'There are better ways of solving things than sending in a gunship!'

PRINCE ALBERT, 1819–1861

8 Explain reasons

'Knowledge which is acquired under compulsion obtains no hold on the mind.'

PLATO, 428–348 BC

Form your child's mind. Put at least as much effort into coaching your child's discernment as you do into Saturday sport. The mind is no less important than the body. We can underplay the role of reason in educational maturing.

> *'My father was accustomed to shape me as a boy by words.'*
>
> HORACE, 65–8 BC

We have already looked briefly at the link between reason and virtue. Cicero spoke of virtue as 'the perfection of reason', meaning that clear thinking needs to lead to good patterns of behaviour – thought is meant to mature into action. The greater self-dominion through reason and good habits, the greater freedom we experience from our own bad habits, and the greater the power we have to resist bad influences in our environment or peer group. Without self-possession, a good life is impossible, and happiness will be sought in illusions.

Translate all this into sound parenting practice:

- Emphasise the importance of sound judgement in life, choices made with sufficient information, and keeping apart emotions and personal prejudices. When you debrief a teenager after you have let them make up their mind, help them recognise decisions based on incomplete information or prejudice. Help children recognise the light research that goes into much television journalism.
- Explain the reasons for many practical lifestyle issues: why they should work hard, why it is not a good idea to try marijuana, why pornography is damaging, how female fashions can affect a male psyche, etc. Make a list.
- Teach your teenager to understand impulsive reactions so as to better control them. Teach about how reason,

emotions and passions interact, and how head should at least approve of emotional reactions. Talk about how antecedent passion, passion that kicks in before we make a conscious decision to run with it, short-cuts rationality.

- Teach critical thinking. Help your child recognise the facts in a situation, and to distinguish feelings and desires from objective information. Teach children to be slow to judge people's intentions, but that they are entitled to form an opinion about external behaviour. Model this.
- Insist on commitments. If Mary elects to play softball, she attends every training and game. If John promises himself to another for life, he means it.

Have the reasons ready

Forearm your teenager for the battles he or she will have to fight to stay on track to happiness. Start with the following principles.

- Life is sacred ... always.
- Truth is to be defended ... always.
- We either live for others or for ourselves.
- We are made for happiness. There is more happiness in giving than receiving.
- Life is about the flourishing of relationships.
- Genuine love always brings commitments and inevitable suffering.
- Feelings may or may not point you in the right direction. Follow your head not your feelings.
- Ask advice.
- Attach yourself to the best people you know.
- Work is service to others.
- Put creativity into your friendships.
- All human beings deserve basic respect regardless of their actions.
- Right and wrong are absolutes.
- The end never justifies the means.
- Love unites, hatred divides.
- Only apologies and forgiveness solve conflict.
- Addictions take away freedom.
- Happiness is not in things.

9 Don't underestimate the impact of the peer group

'All people become like the company they keep.'

EURIPIDES, 485–406 BC

The peer group will always get your kids. At least that was the message of *Nurture Assumption*, a book that came out a few years ago based on a US study. Not pleasant reading.

Without question, teenagers are immensely impressionable. Their friends are *reinforcing* the habits and values you are fostering, or they are *undermining* them. A neutral peer group is not possible.

A positive peer example is priceless in a school, but the inverse is also true. It can break your heart when children dumb themselves down to the group and absorb attitudes of unmotivated friends. It can be so obvious when children are acting out attitudes they take from models outside the family, and you can feel powerless to stop such attitudes seeping in.

The battle to consolidate a positive peer group is most easily won in the childhood years. Choice of school can help, but don't take things for granted. Just one close friend can be the decisive influence on a child, particularly if home connections are tenuous.

Remember also that the sustained example of those around us will always rub off, even as adults. The trick is to play peer group at its own game. Create positive peer groups. Most of us are somewhat like Harriet in Jane Austen's *Emma*, whose 'character depends on those she is with'. Without good friends and without a well-developed spectrum of good habits it is too easy to surrender one's principles, providing only the lamest opposition when the crunch comes. So talk to your children, even when they are very young, about their friends. Help them recognise when family values are in conflict with peer values. Don't breed paranoia, but rather a healthy desire to raise the standard wherever they go.

Classic wisdom: the influence of peer group

'Company of good men is a training in virtue, but the company of bad men is the ruin of it.'

Socrates, 469–399 BC

'A single example of extravagance or greed does a lot of harm. A close friend who leads a pampered life gradually makes one soft and flabby. A wealthy neighbour will make you crave for possessions. A companion with a malicious nature tends to rub off some of his rust even on someone of an innocent and openhearted nature.'

Seneca, 4 BC – 65 AD

Do your kids bring their friends home? Do you find things to admire in each friend, and do you suggest ways that your child can be of service to that friend. Don't shy away from talking to your child about sharing your own family values with that friend if he or she wants. Teach moral leadership; the alternative is not very palatable. Talk openly about the importance of having good friends, and of seeking out the very best teachers in future career paths.

Stealth peer groups

Be especially careful to monitor the negative example that impressionable young people receive.

You know your child's friends and their families, but do you also know who your child is spending time with on the television, who is speaking to them on the radio, who they are online with? Stranger danger comes in many forms.

We must raise children to be masters of their own lives, not to be tossed to and fro by the example of friends and the demands of their tummies. One mother was talking: 'I don't believe this. My son has such a terrible time remembering his spelling, but he can tell me immediately what brand of sports shoes every single one of his classmates wears.' How can hype-marketing succeed when the best tutors and classroom teachers can't make an impression?

10 Look for reinforcement from your son's or daughter's school

'I give them lots of love and tell them that we don't tolerate that behaviour here.'

LOUISIANA REFORM SCHOOL HEADMISTRESS INTERVIEWED ON SYDNEY RADIO

Your son's or daughter's school will either be an effective ally, or it will undermine your best efforts. Just as unity between parents is the key to successful parenting, unity between parents and teachers is the key to successful learning – of every type. School and home must be in step.

When parents and teachers trust each other, children benefit. No teacher should say to a student who is whingeing when the class is given more work, 'Don't blame me, a parent complained.' This would be passing the buck, and not accepting the professional responsibility of maintaining the prestige of parents in the eyes of their children. A teacher should never criticise a parent, let alone ridicule a parent's opinion, above all in front of that parent's child.

The opposite is also true. At the dinner table, parents who smile when children ridicule a teacher send the wrong message. Unchecked backseat conversations making fun of anyone are out of place, let alone conversations which target the adults to whom the parents have entrusted these very children. Parents who criticise their child's teacher should not be surprised when the child loses respect for that teacher's authority. They may convince themselves that the child's *personality clash* with the teacher confirms their own discomfort with a particular teacher, but a child's habitual responses will normally mirror any parental prejudices.

Of course, there can be legitimate concerns. But be aware that the most conscientious and committed parents can be easily drawn *emotionally* into school issues, and as a consequence, their judgement will be clouded. Every teacher comes across experienced parents, perhaps who are great supporters of the school, but who are notoriously bad judges of situations in which their own children are involved. Don't go in with your guns drawn; emotion will spoil your aim.

Does your school …

- see parents as the *first educators*?
- provide excellent support for parents?
- establish strong lines of communication with parents?
- raise the profile of parenting issues, and provide practical input for parents?
- see the character-forming potential in teaching children that all work is a form of service?
- have a staff in which teachers see that their example, and professed values, are crucial?
- effectively develop peer values and example?
- regard discipline and sport essentially as character-forming activities?

Find out the facts first

'Your teacher did what?' You reach for the phone.

Don't take sides when your child complains about treatment from a teacher. This is not to doubt your child; you *also* have a duty to help him or her realise that there are always two sides to a conflict. Too often maternal or paternal instinct leaps into the fray. Remind yourself that teachers and parents have the same goal – the welfare and academic progress of the child.

Kids can be like advertisements: they only tell you the favourable bits of the story. If your daughter tells you that the teacher is picking on her, realise it is not necessarily true just because she has said it before. You may only have half the facts. Talk directly to the teacher. Don't prejudge. Ring and say, 'Please fill me in on what is happening. I heard there was a clash with you today, but I'm sure there is more to this.' One hundred percent of the time you will be right.

'I have never let my schooling interfere with my education.'

MARK TWAIN, 1835–1910

11 Seek out mentors who have the confidence of your teenager

'Mother and nurse and father and tutor are vying with one another about the improvement of the child as soon as ever he is able to understand what is being said to him.'

PLATO, 428–348 BC

In recent days I learnt of two sad situations. A twelve-year-old boy had been introduced to marijuana by an older neighbour. And the daughter of close friends, young for her class group, was swayed by older friends into drugs.

One significant adult outside the home can have a decisive impact on the life development of a young person – for better or for worse. At times parents need to take decisive action, and without getting into arguments, explain why clearly and simply to their child: 'I trust your good intentions, but you do not yet have the experience or judgement to recognise the danger in going to a big after party with friends who have already been drinking for five or six hours.'

How can we apply this wisdom positively? It can be all but impossible to dictate friendships to a teenager. More discreet management is required. For example, careful choice of school and sporting clubs is absolutely necessary. Television guidelines in the home need to be well in place before the years of adolescence kick in. Just because Buffy has been a mentor for a million fourteen-year-old girls, and just because Bart Simpson has been named the most influential teenager in the Western world, that doesn't mean they can come and go in your own lounge room. We must manage the voices talking to children if those voices are unhealthy.

What a terrific advantage it is when your son or daughter has an older friend who they look up to, provided it is an older friend whose advice you trust! For example, for two years you have been asking your son daily to start his homework before dinner, but only when his rugby coach insists on it does it stick. Or you regret the brittle words with your daughter about the suspect suitability of a particular top she wanted to wear; then overnight she adopts the bohemian but thankfully far more decent taste of an adored cousin. Do some creative networking.

The original Mentor

When Odysseus was late home after the Trojan War, his wife Penelope allowed her son to search for him but put the boy under the guidance of a trusted servant, named, predictably, Mentor. That Mentor was actually a god in disguise did not stop the word passing into common usage.

Friends who speak the truth

Marcus Aurelius, in his impressive Meditations, *left us frank writings revealing his determination to be the best person he could be. Also, from his youth, there are beautiful letters which reveal his gratitude and fondness for his foster parents and for his mentor, Fronto, a significant general.*

In one letter he thanks Fronto for his honesty in correcting him whenever necessary. 'Why am I happy? Because I have learnt from you to speak the truth. Your fault findings and your advice have shown me the way without guile and feigned words. You have taught me before all to speak the truth and at the same time to listen for the truth. Farewell my good master, my best of masters. I am overjoyed to call you my friend.'

'Every young thing attaches itself to what is nearest and grows to be like it: the character of the mentor is reproduced in that of the young man.'

SENECA, 4 BC – 65 AD

'Nowadays the common practice of many persons is ridiculous. They will even put their sons in the care of known alcoholics.'

PLUTARCH, 46–120

Yet do not some parents today entrust their children to the mentorship of offensive reality television and appalling video clips?

12 Focus on resilience

'Drag your thoughts away from your troubles; by the ears, by the heels, or any other way you can manage it.'

MARK TWAIN, 1835–1910

It is foolish to disregard the link between indulged children and teenagers who collapse in the face of difficulties. In life we all cope according to the habitual skills that life experience and specific training have engendered. A child who has not had to deal with small challenges may not cope well when the bigger difficulties mount up.

Each generation has to grapple with its own demons, and the Scooter Generation is being assaulted by a culture where feelings and emotions demand immediate gratification. Teenagers can be just as susceptible as younger children, but the stakes are higher; an adolescent ruled by feelings is seriously vulnerable not only to over-spending, but far more problematically, to disproportionate risk-taking, premature sexual experience, substance abuse, eating disorders, and often to anxiety and depression. Pandora's Box flies open.

Marketing to teenagers is about creating wants. Executive careers are built on this. Think of Bart Simpson proclaiming in a thousand bus shelters across the nation: 'I want my Foxtel.' The glossy teen magazines, the television ads, the radio promos all prey on teen consumers who have more disposable income than many adults, but who are woefully short on the life experience needed to make sensible spending choices. The free spending habits of many young people are essentially habits of gratification and impulsiveness.

The more spoilt the child and the more pressing the needs that must be constantly appeased, the greater that child's potential dissatisfaction with life. Socrates was right on the money when he proclaimed, 'That person is happiest who needs least.'

How do we build the resilience in kids so they can handle

whatever life tosses at them, without dodging it and without depression?

1 **Model self-control in all its aspects.** Control your own temper. Curb your appetite. Don't buy on impulse. Limit curiosity. Teach moderation – be prepared to get up from the table eating just a little less than you would like. And keep a smile on your face. Happiness has never been found in losing self-control. Heed Aristotle's dictum: 'The impulses of incontinent people carry them in the opposite direction from that towards which they were aiming.'

2 **Teach problem-solving.** Teach that problems can be fixed. With Marcus Aurelius teach, 'Never let the future disturb you. We will meet it, if we have to, with the same weapons of reason we use to face today.'

3 **Try to live with trust in providence.** Studies show that families with faith and ideals raise children who are more resilient. Can you find in your upbringing habits of prayer that you can reactivate and then pass on to your children?

4 **Help your child to see that failures all have a positive side.** As Steve Waugh said: 'There is no position so hopeless that it could not be regarded as a challenge and so be turned into a positive force'.

Depressed mothers who managed to rise above their melancholy, lavishing their babies with attention and indulging in playful games, had children with brain activity of a considerably more cheerful cast.

RESEARCH BY GERALDINE DAWSON, UNIVERSITY OF WASHINGTON

Depression strikes

We were talking in the staffroom one afternoon about several Year 8 children who had come to school with $50 in their wallet to be slotted away in Timezone. One teacher's response: 'It's amazing these kids carry more money in their pockets than I do!' Another on a teacher's wage quipped, 'That's not amazing, that's depressing!'

13 Prepare your son or daughter for relationships and sexuality

'Always recognise that human individuals are ends, and do not use them as means to your end.'

IMMANUEL KANT, 1724–1804

How do you talk to your child about human love? What a tremendous opportunity to explain the beautiful gift of sexuality and the privilege of being able to bring a new life into the world. Isn't it ironic that many parents prefer to talk about footy, homework, brushing teeth, and a whole myriad of other trivia, but they allow strangers to talk to their children about the most intimate topics. And what a pity, because it is a marvellous opportunity for parents and children to grow closer together! Nobody is better placed than a loving parent to explain to a child that the biology goes with unconditional affection and lifetime commitment.

Personal Development at school may give a good biological explanation but can be very light on the intangibles of commitment, bonding and devotion to family, which must be part of any comprehensive sex and human relationships education. What a mistake to let a streetwise school friend or some television sex show get in first.

I will never forget one parent telling me, 'But Karel is not fourteen yet. Surely it's not time to talk to him about sex!' Get in early. It is far easier to teach a younger boy, by your decisive response to television smut, to respect all women, than to try to convince your teenager that pornography is wrong. It will cause less angst all round to teach a younger girl the decent length of a skirt than to hope to explain the issue to an indignant teenager. If parents do not talk with their younger children about what is acceptable behaviour with a friend of the opposite sex, they may find it very hard to get the message across that serious kissing is out of place for a fifteen-year-old.

Open sex education needs to be a priority in your home well before secondary years. Don't just talk biology, talk about the beauty of committed life-long love and what it takes to achieve that. And don't underestimate the importance of modelling in your own relationship the unconditional service and total consideration that your children will need in their adult relationships.

Do your best to open your home to your children's friends. Great benefits ensue from families networking with other families to create the peer group they want for their children. If you don't naturally have an extended family, try to create one? When youth culture becomes alienated from family life, a certain percentage of children will end up badly damaged.

What to say when

Avoid dramatic one-off chats in which the parent can be far more nervous than the child. Talk personally and honestly. Revisit the conversations to ensure that the lessons are learnt. Why should our televisions talk more frankly to our children than we do?

- By ten, children should have learnt the facts of life from their parents.
- By twelve, talk about some of the adolescent challenges they will face: pornography, misuse of sex as selfish gratification, the duty never to take advantage of anyone, the need to bring their friends home, and so on. If children do not have good habits of self-control, respect for others and modesty by the time they hit teenage years, they will be under-prepared for social life.
- Fewer kids fall into mistakes they have been explicitly warned about, so advice for young teens also needs to be very specific. Talk to your twelve and thirteen-year-old about what is okay in friendships between boys and girls, and what is simply taking advantage of the situation or the other person. Be specific about what behaviour and interaction is proper and what is inappropriate in friendships between boys and girls. It is not a matter of not trusting, but of avoiding having young people land in situations for which they are unprepared.

'Nothing so provokes another to love us than to love them first.'

Augustine of Hippo, 354–430

Help teenagers to be masters of themselves

- Encourage your children to mix with and get to know many, many boys and girls their own age. Teach that the aim of social life cannot simply be to find one girlfriend/boyfriend, with all the emotional obsession premature relationships create. Our young people need to understand the good *reasons* for not pairing off in mid-teen years.
- Talk about how emotions, passions and attachments are *meant* to turn on with frequent meeting, with physical contact or with one-on-one situations.
- Explain how certain uninhibited social venues – raves and some discos particularly – make it much harder for a person to maintain self-possession, because the behaviour there sets a poor standard.
- Explain how certain heady times, such as the weeks after final school exams finish, can put a young person under pressures never before experienced, leading to mistakes they may regret bitterly.
- Explain how sexual relationships create life-strong bonds and why therefore it is wrong to cross this line without lifelong commitments.
- Talk about why marijuana, ecstasy, amphetamines and excessive alcohol are bad news, and how these change our brain and affect our social behaviour. Explain that hours of seemingly mild consumption of alcohol can gnaw away at our willpower and ultimately at our standards of behaviour. For this reason some after parties have a major fallout.
- It is far better to have these conversations before emotions are involved. Every one of us has a gene to justify why we should be allowed to do the things we have set our hearts on.

Serious foundations for the years to come ...

David, four-years-old, asks his dad:

'Daddy, are you going to have another big tummy and a boy?'

Dad thinks quickly, 'No, it's mummy who gets the tummy.'

'No! Mummy has the girls, daddy has the boys.'

***

'Do you know where babies really come from?' Dad asks his son.

'Yeah, Dad, I know it all,' nine-year-old Liam answers.

'You tell me!' Dad counters.

Liam freezes, looking for a way out. 'You just explain it,' he says to his dad with a wave of the hand. A great conversation ensues.

14 Give your teenager affection, affection, and more affection

'Let us always meet each other with a smile, for the smile is the beginning of love, and once we begin to love each other, naturally we want to do something.'

MOTHER TERESA, 1910–1997

The girl is looking away. Her father holds a school report in his hand and is talking to his daughter. The fifteen-year-old tries to answer, scowls in frustration, and turns her whole body. Her father presses on, 'You didn't do any work, so what sort of report did you expect? Wake up to yourself. This term forget about going out, television and chat rooms. I'll have that mobile phone now, thank you very much.'

Is this approach likely to work? Probably not – if dad prefers to speak rather than to listen, if he continues to lecture and to exaggerate, the resentment he causes will be virtually irreparable. While he is blaming his child for the breakdown in rapport, he himself is the cause. He is not only deaf to what his daughter tries to say, but he is blind to his own role in the breakdown.

> *'Govern your children by winning their full respect. Fathers, do not drive your children to resentment.'*
>
> PAUL OF TARSUS

Parents need to be skilful in making home an enjoyable place to be, and the affection they show must be palpable. Affection – shown in the here and now. Know what is in your child's heart and mind. Know what is causing them joy and pain, today. A child with whom we talk little will grow distant.

Affection is always in the immediate present in:

- the expression on your face
- finding one-on-one time to talk
- simple physical contact – have your own signs, a hand on

the shoulder when the late study light is burning, touching heads when something important happens or a serious piece of news arrives
- following up concerns – ask how the test went that was worrying your child the night before
- small acts of service – offer to drop a child at school when he is taking in a bulky project or offer to take over the washing up when your daughter has an assessment task
- small, specific acts of praise and encouragement – know the things your son or daughter does well and look for opportunities to say something positive
- small expressions of confidence – ask a child's opinion, or give specific compliments such as, 'You answered that phone well', 'You do this better than I do; can you read this fine print?'

Give affection even when your son or daughter *seems* not to need it; later on you will need that credit in the account. Give affection even when it is positively rejected – not in annoying, invasive ways, such as a hair tousle when you realise your son is cringing, but through the warmth in your voice and an open, uncomplicated smile. Never take your child's rejections personally; this is just what adolescents do sometimes!

> *'When you link a son to you by kindness, there is sincerity in all his acts, he sets himself to correspond to your love, and he will be the same behind your back as to your face.'*
>
> TERENCE, 190–159 BC

Know how to look beyond personal injury

It is said that Abraham Lincoln once was bowled over by an angry young man running through the corridor. Far from responding angrily, he asked, 'Young man, what's troubling you?' We adults have a duty not to over-react to the impoliteness of children. When we react angrily, the child resents the emotion and misses the correction.

15 Teach peace in the face of the very greatest challenges

'If we have no peace it is because we have forgotten that we belong to one another.'

MOTHER TERESA, 1910–1997

A Year 12 girl was speaking to her Principal after the second tragic death within weeks in their school family: '... I think this is a wake-up call, telling us that here at school we are so protected and happy but we must get ourselves ready to deal with the pain and suffering that is out there'.

This young woman was realising that the crises of childhood are non-events: dented relationships, emotional speed bumps, skin blemishes and tough exams. They are oceans apart from the serious challenges of adult life – irreversible problems with permanent consequences, lasting pain, incomprehensible malice, seemingly wasted lives, betrayed love. Of course life also brings great and beautiful rewards, but there are very sharp thorns, and everyone gets spiked at times.

For a child's mistakes there always seems to be the *undo* button. Whereas 300 years ago 4 children in 10 would die before their fifth birthday, now 99 out of 100 remain alive. Young persons may see wars on television, but the term *harsh consequences* may simply mean not being allowed to stop for a sundae on the way home. In young adulthood, it has all become very different, as if by stealth. Decisions are suddenly being made that will leave the young adult or others affected for life.

A true story. A young man, not yet twenty and just off his P-plates, was behind the wheel of his new Holden ute. He was tearing after a friend in the car ahead. Speeding around a blind curve he veered into the oncoming traffic. The cars had to be cut apart. He was in a coma for weeks and is now seriously impaired; the pregnant mother in the other car died. For all the thought he had of the consequences of what he was doing, he may as well have been a ten-year-old peddling flat out on his BMX. Action without thought can have catastrophic consequences. We adults are not doing a good job preparing children for the very real crocodiles ahead.

Teenagers want to talk about the big topics. In a survey at my school some older teenagers said they relished deep conversations with their mother or father, while others felt very let down when the whole relationship seemed limited to platitudes or to discussion about studies. Don't shy away from talking about illness and death. It is a duty of each parent to prepare their children for *all* the greatest challenges life can throw at them. And in the normal course of things, it will be a parent's privilege, when the time comes, to teach their own children what it means to die well with a loving and trusting heart. It will be your last and perhaps greatest service to your child. Will you be able to do this?

The last task of parenting

Some years ago, a good friend died of an aggressive bowel cancer. He left behind a large young family. When I visited him in his last week, I asked him how he was feeling. I will never forget his brave reply: 'Mate, I'm slipping, but I've never been in better spirits.' His self-control and courtesy during those months of great discomfort inspired us all. He never complained, and his calm fortitude was a great consolation to all.

My friend's example is now part of the great inheritance that his wife, his children and his friends will take through life, and it will fortify them in the challenges they too will face. His demeanour in the face of his approaching death taught us the deepest lessons about life itself: that love and trust bring a peace that not even pain and death can frighten away.

Inner peace, despite external turmoil, is one of the very greatest gifts a parent can give to his or her child. Yet, as one very wise and now very dead Elizabethan said, 'The long habit of living indisposeth us for dying.' If we are not reconciled to the inevitability of death and the need to walk away from our possessions, we will fail in this last great task of parenting.

Will your parenting effectively prepare your children for the very greatest challenges that life will throw at them?

A CHECKLIST FOR RAISING TEENAGERS WITH CHARACTER

We have a positive view of adolescence. We don't focus our attention on the superficial features.
We address the immediate needs of our child.
We are focused on the long-term need to build strong habits and convictions.
We are striving to prepare even younger children for the challenge of thinking for themselves and running their own lives.
We are convinced of our teenage child's potential to do great things for others. This confidence is tangible.
We own up to our innermost values.
We strive to live out the happiness that our values should deliver.
We realise that teenagers change on the inside first.
We keep the focus on having our teenagers think, rather than obliging his or her conformity to our wishes.
We help our son or daughter *internalise* the process of developing good habits.
We are creative in our ways to keep communicating effectively.
We address issues without putting off difficult conversations.
We explain reasons.
We strive to lay foundations for a positive peer group around our son or daughter.
We do our best to work in close partnership with our child's school.
We seek out mentors who have the confidence of our son or daughter.
We keep our focus on building resilient habits of hardiness, problem solving and self-control.
We give our son or daughter a first-class ongoing preparation for relationships and sexuality.
We live up to our duty to provide unconditional daily affection.
We model peace in the face of life's greatest challenges.

Raising teenagers with strength of character

POINTS FOR REFLECTION

- Socrates: '*Children hear what we say, but follow what we do.*' Be honest about your values.
- Your values must make you happy and be seen to make you happy.
- Foster the virtue of sound judgement.
- Foster generosity.

Level of development in your family					**Priority areas**
Well-developed	***Fair to middling***	***Fair***	***Much work needed***	***Non-existent***	

- Show affection.
- Create customs of conversation.
- Look beneath the surface behaviour of your teenager.
- Consult their opinions.
- Don't back off the tough issues.
- Explain reasons but don't get caught in argument.
- Have confidence in prayer.

Final reflections

What a privilege!

'How can it be anything but a pleasure to raise up from the ground a child that has been born of the two of you and to feed and educate it, a physical and mental mirror of yourself ...?'

EMPEROR AUGUSTUS ON ENACTING A LAW ENCOURAGING LARGER FAMILIES

One of my former students gained a cadetship with a particularly altruistic politician in another country. It was an unforgettable three months tiptoeing in foreign corridors of power. On his return I asked him what he would most remember. Without hesitating, he repeated a saying impressed upon him by his mentor, 'The price of privilege is responsibility.' The greater the opportunity, the greater the duty to serve others through the good fortune it brings.

Apply this to parenting. We can be all too aware of the responsibilities of parenting, but it is good to remember that these responsibilities are a *consequence* of the great privilege of raising children.

All this, in the normal course of life, has been given to you as a parent:

- to receive the promise of another human being to live completely dedicated to your welfare
- together, to bring into this world a child or children whose marvellous potential is in your hands
- to discover in this mission, the unique pathway to your own fulfilment and self-improvement as a human being.

What a blessing to lead others to happiness! What a privilege to be co-responsible for all the good that others will do in their lives! Yet sometimes we fail to reflect. Our sense of wonder is impoverished! We miss the bleeding obvious.

Find ways to reflect in an ongoing way on the great privilege! Some people keep a journal. Some people pray. Some parents talk often together about it. A deep wonder at one's own unworthiness must lead inevitably to joy and gratitude. It will bring you closer together as a couple. It will fortify you in the inevitable moments when the going gets tough. It will give you hope when your own failures or the weaknesses of others sap your confidence in the providence of what you are doing. Through it you will become a better support for your spouse and for your children.

'By their love for each other, parents reveal the meaning of God's love for us.'

JOHN PAUL II, 1920–2005

Never forget

A close friend once spoke to me of his joy at the birth of his second boy. As he cradled his new son in his arms, all the physical and mental pain – the death of their previous son hours after birth, his wife's fiendishly difficult pregnancy and the unremitting pressure of his own long hours of work to provide for a growing family – were just wiped away. 'Sitting with my son in my arms while Jane was showering', he said, 'how quickly the whole scene has changed. It is as if a tape of all that has happened has just erased.'

Ancient writers too speak of this moment. Plutarch tells us that Cato the Elder, in the second century before Christ, was present too at the birth of his children: 'As soon as he had a child born, though he never had such urgent business on his hands, unless it were some public matter, he would be by when his wife washed it and dressed it in its swaddling clothes.'

Do you truly honour your own parents?

'Men will deprive their parents of all rights, as they grow old, and people will mock them too, babbling bitter words against them harshly, and without shame in the sight of gods; nor even to their ageing parents will they give back what once was given.'

HESIOD, C. 700 BC

Parenting invites you to a character makeover

'The greatest gift a parent can give a child is the example of struggling to improve oneself.'

James Stenson, school principal and author

We all carry baggage – bad habits from our childhood and less-than-perfect parenting habits acquired since the new generation arrived, habits of reacting too quickly, rejecting a child when it pushes a particular button, punishing without listening, not listening, not giving time. The list can be very long.

As the Emperor Augustus said, we can watch children to learn about ourselves. See in your child the image of your own strengths and shortcomings. Be honest. If your child is short-tempered, is it because you or your spouse has a short fuse? Or if your child lacks respect for others? Or does not seem to work hard? Or is excessively vain? Where do these features come from?

Parenting requires specific skills that we may or may not have come into the job with. It also requires us to think deeply about the values that we wish to pass on to children as the underpinning principles of their behaviour, and how we intend to pass on those values. Good parenting does not happen automatically nor by chance.

Work on three virtues so attractive in a parent

- **Gratitude** Start with loving diligent care for your own parents. Children will imitate what they experience! Gratitude always brings joy.
- **Humility** opens the door to genuine respect. Learn to apologise. Resist the temptation to *possess* a child, or *clone* to accord with your image of yourself.
- **Fortitude** In a comfortable society, fortitude can be the rarest of character qualities. Follow up issues, but not with a hard-nosed demandingness. Unless it is driven by love for others, fortitude is worthless and not a good example for anyone.

Raising a child is a heaven-sent chance to rebuild negative habits, face temperamental deficits and learn some new skills in the process. Don't pass it up. Rid yourself of the bad habits that compromise your example and your interaction with your child. Work on the gloominess, the impulsive comments or the impatience that seem part of your very make-up. Ride out to battle. Day after day walk in that front door with a positive comment for each child. Be determined to devote Saturday mornings to work around the house. Make resolutions for your own particular struggle. Live out the advice of Augustine of Hippo: 'Be always displeased at what you are, if you desire to attain what you are not.'

Teamwork

Never have I met a parent who did not want to be the best parent he or she could be … in principle! But translating good intentions into action, as we have seen, can be another matter.

I know several groups of parents who have set up a schedule of monthly get-togethers when they meet for a parenting discussion over coffee. All parents have strengths in their own family life and all have areas in which they can learn from others.

Parents have habits to learn too

When Chris was about twelve, I remember a day when I was preparing to take a group of children away for the weekend.

With six children and two adults and a dog to fit in, the car was jam packed, including the roof rack, but just as we were loading the horses in the float one of my girls threw a spanner in the works. There was no way her bag was travelling on the roof! We heard how the bugs would get stuck to it and how the dust from the road would coat it (we had to travel part of the way on a dusty dirt road) and how this was not possible. I tried persuasion and all the arguments I could think of. I was somewhat struggling by this stage!

Then Chris appeared in the kitchen and said quietly, 'It doesn't matter, Mummy'. And of course he was right! He had already rearranged the bags so that we were ready to go!

STEPHANIE, MOTHER OF FOUR, AND PROUD OWNER OF ZIMBA, THE WONDER DOG

A life for others

'Men who are not cheerful in the company of their wives, nor join with them in sportiveness or laughter, are thus teaching them to seek their own pleasures apart from their husbands.'

PLUTARCH, 46–120, ADVICE TO A BRIDE AND GROOM

At the funeral of the mother of some good friends, a grandson read a poem she had composed for her children:

'And when I'm gone, don't squabble over houses;
Just look after your spouses ... things are only things.'

This true matriarch was passing on a deeply valued truth. What a priceless message for one's children – that happiness depends not on possessions but on dedication to others, on truly living for others.

If you are serious about devoting your whole existence to addressing the deepest needs of those you love, *you will know what is in their hearts and minds*. Most scrupulously, you will allow your other and better half the freedom to raise any issue or make any suggestion without getting a negative reaction. No topics, neither about money nor bedroom, will be taboo. What do you learn about yourself from those who know you best? Do you listen openly? Have you been listening all these years to their most heartfelt suggestions and requests?

If you want to improve communication, you will create *habits* of communication; *you will set aside time* to chat deeply each week. Work at your unity, creating time to talk over a candlelit dinner once a week after the kids have gone to bed, or walking the block each night having a chat, or reserving one lunchtime weekly. If the communication is not in a weekly routine, it will most likely not happen consistently.

If you truly live for each other, *you will seek to change yourself.* Your acceptance of each other will be unconditional.

If you are wise, *you will invest in the future*. Don't allow yourselves to drift apart. Enjoy doing things together. Create abundant happy memories to tide you through the tougher times. Be physically present to those you love, otherwise the connection can become very crackly!

Ultimately, our family relationships are a school where we learn to give of ourselves – a grand dynamic built into human nature that helps us overcome the all-too-natural habits of self-centredness in all of us. One father in my school captured the idea in this comment, 'It was only when I had my third child that I accepted I could no longer keep corners for myself in my life. I had to be totally dedicated to my family.'

Things to do

- Fix three or four very specific family resolutions – goals that, if they are achieved, will make your parenting more effective. Agree together to give absolute priority to the way you are raising your family, and in the way that you challenge yourselves.
- Write them down.
- Review them *together* regularly in the months ahead. *This is the most important step.*
- Be committed to make any changes in yourselves, individually and as a team, that are needed to make you more effective as parents.

In conclusion

Two quotations encapsulate the argument of this book:

1 '*Happiness is the reward of virtue.*' Anchor your parenting on this one-liner from Aristotle. Good habitual behaviours founded on a loving regard for others are the very building blocks of happiness.

2 '*Character calls forth character.*' Goethe summed it up so simply. If you are prepared doggedly to remake your own character, your children will be the beneficiaries in their characters. You cannot give to others what you do not possess yourself.

Author's notes

Page xii **'This list reflects the work of David Isaacs, an English Professor of Education'**: David Isaacs's seminal work on character is *Character Building: A guide for parents and teachers*, Four Courts Press, Dublin, 1984. This work appeared first in Spanish in 1976.

Page 2 **'Rafael Pich, father of sixteen ...'**: In conjunction with raising sixteen children of his own, Rafael Pich has started schools, parenting organisations and an NGO in Geneva. He carries himself with an authoritative grandfatherly presence and lectures profoundly in the simplest language.

Page 3 **'James Stenson, school principal and author'**: James Stenson, author and educator, is best known for his books, *Upbringing: A Handbook for Parents of Young Children* (Scepter, New York, 1992); and *Compass* (Scepter, New York, 2003), targeting the parental skills needed for building resilient habits in children.

Page 4 **'Studies demonstrate that the 30 percent of Australian children not raised in a home with both natural parents are more likely to suffer disadvantage on every indicator ...'**: Barry Maley's study, *Family and Marriage in Australia* (CIS, Sydney, 2001), presents a weight of stark data demonstrating the statistical disadvantages endured by children raised in homes without both natural parents.

Page 4 **'James Stenson in *Upbringing* insists that unity is the first characteristic of successful parents. Ray Guarendi echoes this principle ...'**: Stenson, James B, *Upbringing: A Handbook for Parents of Young Children*, Scepter, New York, 1992; Guarendi, Ray, *Back to the Family*, Fireside, Simon and Schuster, New York, 1990.

Page 4 **'While pre-teen children blame themselves when mum or dad is shouting, teenagers lose respect for their parents'**: A survey we entitled 'Communication with Parents' completed anonymously by all secondary students in my school strongly suggested that while younger children blamed themselves even if chronically in trouble older children were more likely to sit in judgement on parental lack of self control, parental stress levels, etc. Detailed analysis of the survey is available on request.

Page 5 **'Barbara Holborow, the former Children's Court magistrate, says that about 85 percent of children entering the juvenile justice system come from broken homes'**: Address to Redfield parents, 3 June 2000; notes available on request. When she decided there was too little governmental will to address root causes of juvenile delinquency, Barbara Holborow resigned in protest from her position as Chief Magistrate of the Children's Court in NSW. In the years since she has devoted her considerable energy to programs matching up mentor mums with first-time single mothers.

Page 6 **'Interpersonal rewards (time and affection) are more important than material rewards'**: Barrett, Paula, Address to AHISA National Pastoral Care Conference, Westminster School, Adelaide, 11–14 July 2000.

Page 6 **'Barbara Holborow observed that the great majority of children who came into her courtroom lacked affection in their homes'**: Address to Redfield parents, 3 June 2000; notes available on request.

Page 6 **'Every piece of research on effective childhood socialisation identifies two broad parameters, emotional support (affection) and limit setting ...'**: In his address to 'Leadership in Boys' Education: A National Forum' at the University of Newcastle, 12–13 May 1999, Don Edgar explained this quotation as the simplest of graphs. Parents need to be high on both axes, on affection *and* boundaries and expectations, otherwise their parenting will be compromised. A grasp of this simple reality can change the way parents raise their children.

Page 7 **'Dr Ross Campbell says parents need to learn to give each child focused attention, with eye and physical contact'**: Campbell, Ross, *How to really love your teenager*, Victor Books, Wheaton, 1983.

Page 7 **'Paula Barrett advises of the importance of being positive and encouraging, and avoiding negative refrains ...'**: Barrett, Paula, Address to AHISA National Pastoral Care Conference, Westminster School, Adelaide, 11–14 July 2000.

Page 7 **'In *How to really love your teenager*, Dr Ross Campbell reminds parents that it is their responsibility to "emotionally nourish" their children ...'**: Campbell, Ross, *How to really love your teenager*, Victor Books, Wheaton 1983.

Page 11 **'All parents damage their children ...'**: Albom, Mitch, *The five people you meet in heaven*, Hyperion, New York, 2003.

Page 14 **'Quotes from Barbara Holborow'**: Address to Redfield parents, 3 June 2000; notes available on request.

Page 18 **'Do intervene in situations of moral or physical danger ...'**: This simple guideline for parents to help them decide whether or not they should direct an older child's actions comes from a course on 'Parents and their Adolescent Children' conducted by Prof. David Isaacs, under the auspices of the University of Navarre, in San Francisco in May 1993.

Page 29 **'Psychologist and author Michele Borba claims that it takes a child 21 days of repeating a new behaviour before it takes'**: Michele Borba is one of the new parenting writers in the United States who are now stressing good habits, in both parents and children. She nominates lack of perseverance in correcting bad behaviour as one of the most common faults in a parent. Borba, Michele, *No More Misbehavin'*, Jossey-Bass, San Francisco, 2003.

Page 37 **'Joseph Pieper, a prominent twentieth-century philosopher, described this vision of character as "... one of the great discoveries in the history of man's self-understanding ..."**: Pieper, Joseph, *The Four Cardinal Virtues*, University of Notre Dame Press, Notre Dame, Indiana, 1966.

Page 37 **'Certainly my experience of twenty years close work with hundreds and hundreds of parents and their children ...'**: Redfield College, of which I am principal, was established in 1986 by a board of parents and teachers, the Parents for Education Foundation, with the aim of working as closely as possible with parents in support of their work as primary educators of their children. A human virtues program meshes with the curriculum, and perhaps more importantly parents are provided with practical ongoing support in the form of frequent parenting seminars and regular personal meetings with the mentor of their child to help them proactively plan their parenting goals. A Catholic priest now canonised, St Josemaria Escriva, was the ultimate inspiration behind many schools similar to Redfield in Europe, the Americas, Africa and Asia. Upon them we have modelled ourselves. In the 1950s and 60s he was encouraging parents to find schools that could give them every support or to found such schools themselves.

Page 41 **'Our habitual actions sum up the sort of person we are'**: Aristotle described how good and bad habits become part of one's very personality. Our habitual actions *determine* who we are. A person who lives *in a state* of infidelity has made himself or herself an adulterer, a person who *habitually* steals makes of himself a thief. Our habits determine the *quality* of our character. One contemporary commentator explains: 'The Greek philosopher Aristotle defined good character as the life of right conduct – right conduct in relation to other persons and in relation to oneself. Aristotle reminds us of what in modern times we are prone to forget: the virtuous life includes self-orientated virtues (such as self-control and moderation) as well as other-orientated virtues (such as generosity and compassion), and the two kinds of virtue are connected.' Palmour, J, *On Moral Character: A Practical Guide to Aristotle's Virtues and Vices*, The Archon Institute for Leadership Development, Washington DC, 1986.

Page 43 **'Top 10 qualities for strong character'**: Lickona, Dr T, *Character Matters: How to help our children develop good judgment, integrity, and other essential virtues*, Simon and Schuster, New York, 2004, pp. 8–11.

Page 66 **'Research tells us that your child will be happier and more resilient with ideals and spiritual beliefs'**: Michael Resnick's major study published in the *Journal of the American Medical Association* demonstrated that children raised in homes teaching a religious faith and/or strong moral principles are less likely to get into drugs, binge drinking, sexual promiscuity and self-harming behaviours. He also documented a correlation between domestic discord and adolescent depression. A conviction in the world of the spirit is surely an antidote to the materialism of our age. Despite all our wealth and comfort, a time will come when we each will have to let go. Without spiritual convictions we can see only an inevitable loss of loved ones and personal oblivion. Resnick, M D, et al., 'Protecting adolescents from harm: findings from the National Longitudinal Study on Adolescent Health', *Journal of the American Medical Association*, vol. 278, no. 10, 1997, pp. 823–32.

Page 67 **'Take conversation seriously ...'**: Paper presented at 'Building Critical Relationships for Children and Youth', a conference organised by PRODEC, University of Western Sydney, 4 July 1998. Associate Professor Sue Dockett's work at the University of Western Sydney has been outstanding in this regard. Her transcripts of conversations with young children demonstrate the depth of communication possible when the adult is prepared to connect.

Page 71 **'Possible jobs for a seven-year-old child'**: This list of jobs was generated in workshops with parents of seven-year-old students. Parents compared notes about what jobs they were asking of their seven-year-olds. The discrepancies were amazing. Some had their children cooking and vacuuming every week, others had no jobs at all.

Page 72 **'Dr Donald DeMarco explains that strengths of character empower us to love others effectively. His *Heart of Virtue* is a collection of wonderful stories to illustrate virtues'**: DeMarco, Donald, *The Heart of Virtue*, Ignatius, San Francisco, 1996.

Page 72 **'Caritas'**: Augustine's caritas extended to love of God. He taught that self-serving actions can deprive us of happiness in this life and in the next; they fail others, and they give no glory to the Creator.

Page 75 **'Child psychologist Michele Borba says, "The best way to stop an inappropriate behaviour is by getting at the root of the problem ..."'**: Borba, Michele, *No More Misbehavin'*, Jossey-Bass, San Francisco, 2003.

Page 76 **'Keep checking for the "learned helplessness" that Martin Seligman first spotted on the radar screen'**: Seligman, Martin, *The Optimistic Child*, Houghton Mifflin Company, New York, 1995.

Page 77 **'The Emperor Augustus asked a great deal of his adopted sons: "When they were still young, he gave them political responsibility ..."'**: Suetonius, *The Twelve Caesars*, The Folio Society, London, 1964.

Page 80 **'For Stephen Covey, conscience is not religious jargon ...'**: Covey, Stephen, *The 7 Habits of Highly Effective Families*, Allen & Unwin, New York, 1997.

Page 82 **'Early childhood studies are showing how important early experience is in children's learning'**: Schwartz, J M & Begley, S, *The Mind and the Brain*, Harper Collins, New York, 2003.

Page 82 **'As James Stenson wryly says, "Pay now or pay later, but either way you pay"'**: Conversation with author in New York, 1993.

Page 82 **'Children who don't play much, or are rarely touched, develop brains 20 percent to 30 percent smaller than normal for their age'**: 'By the age of three, a child who is neglected or abused bears marks that, if not indelible, are exceedingly difficult to erase.' Nash, J Madeleine, 'Fertile minds', *Time Magazine*, 3 February 1997, pp. 36–46.

Page 89 **'Professor David Isaacs says, "Generous people act unselfishly and cheerfully for the benefit of others ..."'**: Isaacs, David, *Character Building: A guide for parents and teachers*, Four Courts Press, Dublin, 1984.

Page 96 **'But ACER research gives some cause for concern that positive civic attitudes are not being effectively fostered in Australian children'**: Schools and the Social Development of Young Australians, ACER, 1998. The study involved 2646 teachers and 8144 students across Australia in Years 5 and 10, and it seems to reveal wide cracks in the ethical education of students. For example, its authors found that only 23 percent of Year 10 students endorsed 'helping someone who is less well off than you', and only 40 percent believed that 'looking after someone who is not well or upset' is important. So let's not kid ourselves that ideals and altruism are at record levels in our schools.

Page 97 **'Professor David Isaacs insists that "Your child must experience the joy that comes from serving others"'**: From a course on 'Parents and their Adolescent Children' conducted by Prof. David Isaacs, under the auspices of the University of Navarre, in San Francisco in May 1993.

Page 103 **'Advertisers and the media can be "rivals for your children's hearts and minds"'**: This comes from a short, spot-on article by James Stenson, 'Born to serve, not to shop', available through < www.parentleadership.com >.

Page 107 **'The two discoveries of adolescence'**: Outlined at a course on 'Parents and their Adolescent Children' conducted by Prof. David Isaacs, under the auspices of the University of Navarre, in San Francisco in May 1993.

Page 111 **'It is the duty of a parent to give emotional support to a child'**: Campbell, Ross, *How to Really Love Your Teenager*, Victor Books, Wheaton, 1983.

Page 112 **'Dr Judith Rapoport and her colleagues were surprised to discover bursts of grey matter building in the first MRI longitudinal study of teenagers' developing brains'**: Giedd, J N, Rapoport, J L, Blumenthal, J, Jeffries N O, et al., 'Brain development during childhood and adolescence: a longitudinal MRI study', *Nature Neuroscience*, vol. 2, no. 10, 1999, pp. 861–3.

Page 124 **'Many parent-child relationships take their pear shape far into adult years'**: The path-breaking work of Robert Bly in this area is notable: Bly, Robert, *Iron John*, Addison Wesley, Boston, 1990.

Page 127 **'Help your teenager internalise the process of developing good habits'**: John Paul II developed this concept in his 1994 *Letter to Families*: 'The process of education ultimately leads to the phase of self education, which occurs when the individual, after attaining an appropriate level of psycho physical maturity, begins to "educate himself on his own". In time, self education goes beyond the earlier results achieved by the educational process, in which it continues to be rooted. An adolescent is exposed to new people and new surroundings, particularly teachers and classmates, who exercise an influence over his life which can be either helpful or harmful. At this stage he distances himself somewhat from the education received in the family, assuming at times a critical attitude with regard to his parents. Even so, the process of self education cannot fail to be marked by the educational influence which the family and school have on children and adolescents. Even when they grow up and set out on their own path, young people remain intimately linked to their existential roots.'

Page 129 **'Consensus on effective parent-child communication'**: These points are found in Ray Guarendi's *Back to the Family* (Fireside, Simon and Schuster, New York, 1990), a best-selling treasure of sound parenting practice generated by Guarendi's interviews with families nominated by award-winning teachers across all the states of the USA.

Page 135 **'At least that was the message of *Nurture Assumption*, a book that came out a few years ago based on a US study'**: Harris, Judith Rich, *The Nurture Assumption*, Free Press, New York, 1998.

Page 137 **'Look for reinforcement from your son's or daughter's school'**: Macbeth's ground-breaking study entitled *The Child Between* (Commission of the European Communities, Education Series 13, Brussels, 1984) put school-home partnerships on the agenda in Europe. Two excellent resources for schools are Thomas Lickona's *Educating for Character: How our schools can teach respect and responsibility* (Bantam Books, New York, 1991), and Kevin Ryan and Karen Bohlin's *Building Character in Schools* (Jossey-Bass, San Francisco, 1999). Both books are authored by directors of major character education centres servicing schools: New York University's Centre for the 4th and 5th Rs, and Boston University's Centre for the Advancement of Character and Ethics.

Page 140 **'The original Mentor'**: Mentoring is no new discovery. In classical times, careful parents took much more effort than we sometimes do to link their children with responsible older role-models. The Romans saw a mentor, or paedogogue, as he was called, as a type of ideal big brother (neither in the Orwellian nor reality TV sense). The great essayist, Plutarch, wrote that the tutor should 'train the child's character to take a first step as it were, on the path to virtue'. And another writer says that discerning Roman parents chose their closest and most faithful friends to be mentors of their children. Another said that, above all, the tutor must be a 'bonus vir', a good man. Then, as now, this was not always the case. Plutarch warned his fellow Romans against allowing their children to associate with others indiscriminately, a trap into which we too can fall.

Page 142 **'Studies show that families with faith and ideals raise children who are more resilient'**: Resnick, M D, et al., 'Protecting adolescents from harm: findings from the National Longitudinal Study on Adolescent Health', *Journal of the American Medical Association*, vol. 278, no. 10, 1997, pp. 823–32.

Page 142 **'Depressed mothers who managed to rise above their melancholy, lavishing their babies with attention and indulging in playful games, had children with brain activity of a considerably more cheerful cast'**: Nash, J Madeleine, 'Fertile minds', *Time Magazine*, 3 February 1997, pp. 36–46.

Acknowledgements

Some years ago now, to his students at Marcellin College in Randwick, Br John Baptist inculcated a love of classical literature and expression. This opportunity to distill the wisdom of so many into only a few pages finds its origins in those first floor Latin classes in the old school building. Without the timeless authority of the Homers, Virgils and Plutarchs, and without the great writings on virtue education in a line from Aristotle to Aquinas, this book would be little better than a parade of shallow opinions.

This book also owes much to insights from the work of many contemporary authorities on parenting and character education. Foremost, Professor David Isaacs, James B Stenson, Rafael Pich and Joe Arevalo have willingly shared their own knowledge. The work and encouragement of Dr Thomas Lickona, of State University of New York, Cortland, have also meant a great deal. I have found the writings of John Paul II on the human person, and on the family and relationships, inspirational.

The Parents for Education Foundation, the board of Redfield College, has shown vision in bringing numerous overseas speakers to Australia and in promoting study tours to the USA and Europe. The insights and experiences of so many parents over twenty years in Redfield have enriched these pages and I owe a particular debt to my colleagues, Frank Monagle, James Burfitt, Gary Steller and Martin Fitzgerald. And in some way, the parents, staff and students of Redfield College, Bidwill High School, Pittwater High School and Sydney Technical High School are also present in these pages. Also, I am very grateful to friends who have contributed stories from their own family life, or who have offered suggestions on the manuscript. Without the crucial editorial contributions of Rex Finch, Sean Doyle and Kathryn Lamberton this work would be formless, if not spineless, literally.

Lastly, were it not for the writings on education and parenting of Josemaria Escriva, a priest now canonised by the Catholic Church, I doubt that I would have discovered teaching, nor have even caught a glimpse of the privilege it is to help a young person build up the character that will bring them happiness in adult life.

ANDREW MULLINS

Recommended reading

General parenting

Covey, Stephen, *The 7 Habits of Highly Effective Families*, Allen & Unwin, New York, 1997.

Guarendi, Ray, *Back to the Family*, Fireside, Simon and Schuster, New York, 1990.

Guarendi, Ray, *You're a Better Parent than You Think*, Fireside, Simon and Schuster, New York, 1998.

Hawkes, Dr Tim, *Boy, Oh Boy: How to raise and educate boys*, Prentice Hall, Sydney, 2001.

Holborow, Barbara, *Those Tracks on My Face*, Random House, Sydney, 1996.

Holborow, Barbara, *Kids: Loving for Life*, Random House, Sydney, 1999.

Seligman, Martin, *The Optimistic Child*, Houghton Mifflin Company, New York, 1995.

Character education

Aristotle, *Ethica Nicomachea*.

Bennett, William, *The Book of Virtues*, Bookman Press, Melbourne, 1994.

Bennett, William, *The Moral Compass*, Bookman Press, Melbourne, 1996.

Borba, Michele, *No More Misbehavin'*, Jossey-Bass, San Francisco, 2003.

DeMarco, Donald, *The Heart of Virtue*, Ignatius, San Francisco, 1996.

Grant, Ian, *Fathers Who Dare Win*, Pa's Publishing, Rozelle, 1999.

Isaacs, David, *Character Building: A guide for parents and teachers*, Four Courts Press, Dublin, 1984.

John Paul II, *Familiaris Consortio*, 1979.

John Paul II, *Letter to Families*, 1994.

Kilpatrick, William, *Why Johnny Can't Tell Right from Wrong*, Touchstone, Simon and Schuster, New York, 1992.

Kreeft, Peter, *Back to Virtue: Traditional Moral Wisdom for Modern Moral Confusion*, Ignatius Press, San Francisco, 1986.

Lickona, Thomas, *Raising Good Children*, Bantam Books, New York, 1983.

Lickona, Thomas, *Character Matters: How to Help Our Children Develop Good Judgment, Integrity, and Other Essential Virtues*, Simon and Schuster, New York, 2004.

O'Donnell, Margaret and Gerard, *Family Values*, St Pauls, Sydney, 1993.

Pieper, Joseph, *The Four Cardinal Virtues*, University of Notre Dame Press, Notre Dame, Indiana, 1966.

Stenson, James B, *Upbringing: A Handbook for Parents of Young Children*, Scepter, New York, 1992.

Stenson, James B, *Lifeline*, Scepter, New York, 1996.

Stenson, James B, *Compass*, Scepter, New York, 2003.

Older children

Campbell, Ross, *How to Really Love Your Teenager*, Victor Books, Wheaton, 1983.

Carr-Gregg, Michael, and Shale, Erin, *Adolescence: A guide for parents*, Finch, Sydney, 2001.

Castillo, Gerard, *Teenagers and Their Problems*, Four Courts Press, Dublin, 1986.

Donaghy, Bronwyn, *Leaving Early*, Harper Health, Sydney, 1997.

Fuller, Andrew, *Raising Real People: Creating a resilient family*, 2nd edn, Australian Council for Educational Research, Melbourne, 2002.

Children and schooling

Heenan, John, *Cornerstone Values – A Values Education Curriculum*, New Zealand Foundation for Character Education, Invercargill, 1996.

Lickona, Thomas, *Educating for Character: How our schools can teach respect and responsibility*, Bantam Books, New York, 1991.

Ryan, Kevin, and Bohlin, Karen, *Building Character in Schools*, Jossey-Bass, San Francisco, 1999.

Interesting research

Himmelfrab, Gertrude, *The Demoralization of Society*, Institute of Economic Affairs, London, 1995.

Macbeth, A, *The Child Between: Report on School-Family Relationships in the Countries of the European Economic Communities*, Commission of the European Communities, Education Series 13, Brussels, 1984.

Maley, Barry, *Family and Marriage in Australia*, CIS, Sydney, 2001.

Schwartz, J M & Begley, S, *The Mind and the Brain*, Harper Collins, New York, 2003.

Web resources on character building and parenting

www.bbc.co.uk/parenting (Comprehensive but mixed in quality)

www.bu.edu/education/caec/ (Centre for the Advancement of Character and Ethics, Boston University)

www.character.org/ (The Character Education Partnership is a US coalition of organisations and individuals committed to character building)

www.charactercounts.org/ (Another vast gathering of organisations committed to character education giving access to useful links and resources)

www.cornerstonevalues.org (A New Zealand organisation promoting character education in schools)

www.cortland.edu/character (Thomas Lickona's Centre for the 4th and 5th Rs, State University of New York, Cortland – excellent resources and an e-library of further links)

www.dadsden.net (Directed specifically at fathers)

http://community.wa.gov.au/Resources/Parenting/ (Western Australian state government comprehensive parenting website)

www.forbetterlife.org/ (The Random Acts of Kindness Foundation)

helpline@youngmedia.org.au (Young Media Australia's Parent Media Helpline)

www.iamyourchild.org (Website of a US peak parent body)

http://islamic-world.net/mnoc/parentingarticles.htm (Islamic site strong on common sense parenting)

www.learningpeace.com (Useful resources on anger management)

www.micheleborba.com (Very practical tips from a clinical psychologist working from a habit-building perspective)

www.parenting.org.nz (Parenting with Confidence, a dynamic New Zealand based character education foundation)

www.parentingbookmark.com (A wide selection of character-focused articles)

www.parentleadership.com (James Stenson's downloadable resources)

www.racp.edu.au (Provides access to excellent media management resources for parents)

Note: Readers are invited to email the author <andrew.mullins@redfield.nsw.edu.au> with comments on any topics raised in *Parenting for Character*.

Index